Ashtoreth:
Goddess of ~~Love~~ Lust

an exposé by Gwen R. Shaw

Engeltal Press
PO Box 447
Jasper, ARK 72641
Telephone +1 (870) 446-2665
www.engeltalpress.com

ISBN 978-0-9846355-1-1

Printed in the United States of America

Table of Contents

Introduction

For several years, this message of Ashtoreth has laid heavily on my heart. I felt that the Holy Spirit wanted me to get it out to the Church. I knew it would be controversial, so I waited for someone else to do it. But the Church has been silent. Maybe they were blind, maybe they were not strong enough to bear the blows that would come as a result of bringing this subject into the light. It seems that too many want to preach a message that will "tickle" the itching ears.

Paul urged Timothy in 2 Timothy 4:1-4, "*I charge thee therefore before God, and the Lord Jesus Christ, who shall judge the quick and the dead at his appearing and his kingdom; Preach the word; be instant in season, out of season; reprove, rebuke, exhort with all longsuffering and doctrine. For the time will come when they will not endure sound doctrine; but after their own lusts shall they heap to themselves teachers, having itching ears; And they shall turn away their ears from the truth, and shall be turned unto fables.*

And then, again, it is hard to preach against a sin that you, yourself, are ensnared in! A drowning man can't save a drowning man!

Anyone who is first with a truth or a revelation is like a soldier who is placed in the front line where the battle is the fiercest. Throughout Church History men and women have suffered and died to bring truths back into the Church.

Never have Church leaders been under greater attack from the "roaring lion" than right now. It seems like Satan has organized a *"Blitzkrieg"* against the most anointed leaders of our day. He wants to destroy their honour, their works, and their credibility. He is bringing his "big guns" out of his armoury, and Ashtoreth certainly is one of the most powerful "cannons" he has.

This little book is one which every Christian should read, for if Satan can destroy the leaders, he will destroy the families, and destroy the effectiveness of the Christian witness in a world that is without godly morals.

Gwen R. Shaw

Chapter 1

The Kingdom of Darkness

Whenever God is getting ready to do something new and wonderful, the devil raises opposition. During my many years on the mission field, I noticed that every time there was a new move of the Holy Spirit, that was bringing a fresh awakening to the Church, there would be a revival of Buddhism. The Buddhist priests even "stole" our choruses, and substituted other words.

For example, in Taiwan, a popular chorus we used to sing in outdoor revival meetings was:

Come, believe in Jesus,
Come, believe in Jesus,
Come, believe in Jesus right now;
Right now, come, believe in Jesus,
Come, believe in Jesus right now.

He will save you,
He will save you,
He will save you right now
Right now, he will save you,
He will save you right now.

He will heal you, etc.

The Buddhist priests changed the name of Jesus to Buddha, and sang the same words to the same melody.

Sometimes when there was a move of God among the people, a bigger statue of Buddha was erected in the town. The devil is not going to hand over his kingdom and power without a big fight. Jesus called him, "The prince of the world" John 14:30 says: *"Hereafter I will not talk much with you: for the prince of this world cometh, and hath nothing in me."*

The Message Bible puts it this way: *"I'll not be talking with you much more like this because the chief of this godless world is about to attack. But don't worry—he has nothing on me, no claim on me."*

Saint Peter tells us in 1 Peter 5:8, *"Be sober, be vigilant; because your adversary the devil, as a roaring lion, walketh about, seeking whom he may devour."*

Saint John writes concerning the end-times in his prophetic letter to the church in Revelation 12:12, *"Woe to the inhabiters of the earth and of the sea! for the devil is come down unto you, having great wrath, because he knoweth that he hath but a short time."*

Later, in His last sermon to His disciples, Jesus said that the prince of the world has already been judged (John 16:11). He has not only been judged, but has also been sentenced by the Almighty; he just hasn't begun to serve his sentence yet. But we are told already what the sentence is in Revelation chapter 20:1-15. Here we can know the whole story of what will happen to Satan and his demons, who are his eternal slaves.

When John was given the end-time revelations on the Isle of Patmos, he saw the Angel of God unlock "the Well of the Abyss." Out of it came billows of smoke, in such large quantities, that the air was filled with it to such a degree, that the sun was blocked out (Rev. 9:1-2). Mingled with the black smoke were 200 million demon spirits, which the scriptures call "horsemen." They were given an allotted time to bring plagues upon all who *repented not of the works of their hands, that they should not worship devils, and idols of gold, and silver, and brass, and stone, and of wood: which neither can see, nor hear, nor walk: Neither repented they of their murders, nor of their sorceries, nor of their fornication, nor of their thefts"* (Revelation 9:20-21).

These are the days Jesus was referring to when He said: *"It will seem like all Hell has broken loose—sun, moon, stars, earth, sea, in an uproar and everyone all over the world in a panic, the wind knocked out of them by the threat of doom, and the powers-that-be quaking. And then—then!—they'll see the Son of Man welcomed in grand style—a glorious welcome! When all this starts to happen, up on your feet. Stand*

*tall with your heads high. Help is on the way! ....
Be on your guard. Don't let the sharp edge of your
expectation get dulled by parties and drinking and
shopping. Otherwise, that Day is going to take you by
complete surprise, spring on you suddenly like a trap,
for it's going to come on everyone, everywhere at once.
So whatever you do, don't go to sleep at the switch.
Pray constantly that you will have the strength and
wits to make it through everything that's coming and
end up on your feet before the Son of Man"* (Luke
21:25-28, 34-36 *The Message Bible*).

Origin of Demonic Spirits

After Lucifer and one third of the angels rose up
in rebellion against God, instigated war in Heaven,
and were defeated, The Almighty God, Creator,
Preserver, and Final Judge cast them out of Heaven.
Peter speaks of these evil angels: *"...God spared not
the angels that sinned, but cast them down to Hell, and
delivered them into chains of darkness, to be reserved
unto judgment"* (2 Peter 2:4). Those fallen angels lost
their glory, beauty, and heavenly estate. They became
demons who introduced great sins to the people of
Noah's time. They plundered the inhabitants of the
earth, raped the women and girls, introduced sodomy,
and other sexual perversions through their perverse
sexual nature. They also murdered, and brought in
many evil inventions. They even had the ability to

bypass the normal God-given order of procreation and bring forth seed like themselves, called giants.[1] *"And it came to pass, when men began to multiply on the face of the earth, and daughters were born unto them, that the sons of God saw the daughters of men that they were fair; and they took them wives of all which they chose. And the LORD said, My spirit shall not always strive with man, for that he also is flesh: yet his days shall be an hundred and twenty years. There were giants in the earth in those days; and also after that, when the sons of God came in unto the daughters of men, and they bare children to them, the same became mighty men which were of old, men of renown."*[2] (Genesis 6:1-5). The word "giant" comes from the Hebrew *nephil*, i.e. a bully or tyrant; giant. *Nephil* comes from the root word *nephal*—to scatter, to fall, cast down, die, fall, fall away, fugitive, inferior,

---

1   "... for many angels* of God accompanied with women, and begat sons that proved unjust, and despisers of all that was good, on account of the confidence they had in their own strength, for the tradition is that these men did what resembled the acts of those whom the Grecians did call giants.

[* "This notion that the fallen angels were, in some sense, the fathers of the old giants, was the constant opinion of antiquity."]

   Josephus Flavius, *Josephus—The Complete Works*, trans. William Whiston, (Nashville, Thomas Nelson Publishers, 1998) *Antiquities of the Jews,* Book 1, chapter 3:1.

2   Renown: "the condition of being known or talked about by many people" (*Oxford English Dictionary*).

   "Emphasis should be placed upon the fact that they were men of violence who had no respect for other men." Footnote in *Hebrew Greek Key Word Study Bible*, KJV (Chattanooga, AMG Publishers, 1984).

be judged ..." (*Strong's Exhaustive Concordance*). These giants were known as *Nephilim*.[3]

Demonic Spirits Are Being Released in the End-time

There has never been such a strong, powerful, spirit of lust released in the world as there is now. This spirit is in advertising, the radio, the television; it is in music, the arts and the style of today's clothing. It is in everything. God help us!

According to 2 Peter 2:4 multitudes of demons were bound in chains of darkness until the Day of Judgment. Surely that day must be nearly upon us. In Revelation chapter nine, John saw multitudes of demons being released to cause terrible, painful plagues upon mankind and nations who have not repented of their idolatry, their murder (including abortion, the murdering of innocent souls), sorceries, fornication, or thefts, and many others (Rev. 9:18-21).

This generation has felt the greatest onslaught of demonic attacks that the world has ever seen since the days of Noah. Our children are being born into a time which Jesus must have been thinking about when He said: *"And woe unto them that are with*

---

3   For more information on the Nephilim, read: *The Nephilim Agenda* by Randy Demain (Maricopa, XP Publishing, 2010). See book ads page 125.

*child, and to them that give suck in those days! ...
For then shall be great tribulation, such as was not
since the beginning of the world to this time, no, nor
ever shall be"* (Matthew 24:19, 21).

My generation never had to face the evil which
our children and grandchildren experience. I pity
them. Every devil from Hell seems to have risen up
against them to destroy this last generation. In the
last hundred years, there have been two world wars,
and many other great wars which have involved
much of the world, such as the Japan-China War,
the Korean War, the Vietnam War, Desert Storm,
the second Iraq war (which never seems to end), the
Afghanistan war, and now the civil wars in many of
the Muslim nations. I haven't got time or space to
mention the many African and European wars.

Millions of our youth lie dead in some foreign
grave. And worse is yet to come as the demonic
spirits invade nation after nation, government after
government, church after church, and home after
home. It seems as if the world is falling apart. And the
Church isn't fasting and praying, or doing spiritual
warfare, like it should. The pastors are not warning
the people of these end-time demons, or teaching
them how to put on the whole spiritual armour of
God, that will enable them to stand against the wiles
of the devil.

Paul admonished the Church of Ephesus, *"Put
on the whole armour of God, that ye may be able to*

stand against the wiles of the devil. For we wrestle not against flesh and blood, but against principalities, against powers, against the rulers of the darkness of this world, against spiritual wickedness in high places. Wherefore take unto you the whole armour of God, that ye may be able to withstand in the evil day, and having done all, to stand" (Ephesians 6:11-13).

Many kinds of demons have attacked all of mankind. Everyone is suffering from demonic attacks in one way or another. It is impossible to fight against them with natural weapons of flesh and blood. This is a spiritual war. It is costly. It takes prayer and fasting, and living a holy life.

Howard Pittman, in his powerful little book, *Demons: an Eye-Witness Account*[4] tells about the vision he had when his spirit left his body in a near death experience in 1979. He has spoken at our End-Time Handmaidens *International School of Ministry*, and I can verify that he is a man of honour, who served in the New Orleans and Louisiana State Police Departments. God brought him back from his near death experience to live for many years in order to teach us these truths about principalities, powers, and rulers of the darkness of this world, that are trying to destroy it and take millions of souls into Hell.

---

4   *Demons: an Eyewitness Account* by Howard O. Pittman. (Foxworth, Philadelphian Publishing House, 1995). See book ads page 124.

He told us about the five most powerful and most active ranks of demons that we are facing, as they strive to prepare the world for the Antichrist. They are:

1. **The demons of war:** This group is Satan's "cream of the crop," his highest rank and ruling order. "From this group comes all his princes who are the rulers of darkness (Ephesians 6:12), and who are the rulers of principalities. They control spiritual wickedness in high places (Luke 22:53)."[5] They appeared like giant athletes, dressed like Roman soldiers of Bible times. Their job is to instigate wars.

2. **The demons of greed, hate, lust, and strife:** Brother Pittman saw the demon of greed, the second in command. He appeared to be an average, portly man, well-dressed in a business suit—a "good old boy." The work of this demon is to bring economical destruction on the nations of the world through selfishness and greed in the hearts of men.

Demons of hate and strife orchestrate all types of conflict, breaking up of relationships, and fighting. They rule from the international level right down to creating church-splits, causing divorces and family strife.

The ruling spirit of lust works in conjunction with others to break down the conscience of man, to make

---

5   Pittman, *Demons: An Eyewitness Account*, page 22.

him compromise his inbuilt ethics, seducing him to commit immoral acts.

3. **The demons of parapsychology and witchcraft:** "Demons from the third order appeared to be part man—part animal, resembling figures of Greek Mythology." This was illustrated as Pan, the satyr (half man, half goat), and a mermaid. These are the demons who lead men into all things satanic: Satan worship, witchcraft, sorcery, magic, false religions (including eastern mystical religions), cults, the occult, drugs, self-destruction, hypnosis, and an interest in every thing considered "paranormal," including ghosts.

4. **The mystery demon:** This demon hides itself from view and causes a person to be secretive about their sin, hiding that part of their personality. It is the one demon that can possess children before the age of accountability. The illustration for this demon was a little boy torturing a kitten, overshadowed by the mystery demon. The boy appeared to be a normal, lovable child—and probably he was, but this demon that was hidden in him only manifested itself at certain times. It is another type of end-time insanity, of which there are many, with many different names caused by this mystery spirit.

5. **The demons of sexual lust and sexual perversion:** This type of spirit had many different shapes and forms, some repulsive and despicable.

They are the lowest rank Howard Pittman was shown, the "untouchables," and are despised by other demons. This last group works closely with the ruling spirit of lust from the second group.

One that he saw looked like a misshapen frog, almost as large as a human. It was positioned between a man and a woman, and as they were talking together, it moved towards the man's face and "like a puff of smoke" disappeared into the man and he was possessed. This demon's area of expertise is to break down sexual morality. It makes itself look beautiful and desirable to men and women, to make them embrace it with their sovereign will, then it can enter them and lead them into more destruction.[6]

The Spirit of Lust

As I said, the most powerful demon ruling the airwaves and the media today is the spirit of lust. It has become such a strong spirit that sex is used to advertise just about everything on sale, including cars. There are magazines to seduce women, and magazines to seduce men. This spirit has even begun to seduce our children at an early age through music, TV, movies, video games, children's and teenage magazines and the clothing styles on sale. Most of our children don't have the childhood they should have; the spirit of lust is stealing it from them.

6   Pittman, *Demons, An Eyewitness Account*, pages 21-55.

Pornography[7] is available on the Internet via your computer. I am in my eighties, and I see advertisements flashed onto my computer that offend my spirit. I don't want to read that garbage. We are being raped by the world. We are sick and tired of it. They are trying to seduce us, to scar our conscience, to take away the purity of our soul and rob us of the holiness of God, which He has imparted into our lives through the Holy Spirit and His work of sanctification.

Besides the five end-time ruling spirits, mentioned previously, there are many more. They are busy, working day and night in many ways. Volumes could be written about them, but in this message, which God has put on my heart I want to emphasize only one—the ruling spirit of lust: Ashtoreth.

7   See Appendix B, page 103.

Chapter 2

Ashtoreth: The Queen of Heaven and Ruler of Hearts

I want to introduce you to the so-called "Queen of Heaven." Her name is Ashtoreth. Some have called Mary, the mother of Jesus, "The Queen of Heaven," but Mary never referred to herself by that title, and neither do the Holy Scriptures.

The following story was shared with me by one of the Lord's servants, who has served God for many years. He is a preacher, Bible teacher, and a prophet who is highly respected around the world. He is a man who walks very close to God. He spends many hours a day in prayer, and is a man who lives a clean, holy, pure and chaste life before the Lord. I have known him many years. He has a burden for, and has preached the Gospel in, forbidden nations. He has been willing to lay down his life many times in great danger for the Lord Jesus. He has followed closely in the footsteps of Sadhu Sundar Singh, the great missionary martyr from India who has gone to be with the Lord. This man of God never travels alone, as he feels that the Lord wants him to be accompanied by a brother in Christ, an intercessor, who always prays for him while he is preaching. Jesus also sent His disciples out two by two.

He told me that one day an unexpected visitor appeared before his intercessor in the shape of a very, very beautiful woman. This woman was so incredibly attractive, that the intercessor said that he had never before seen such an exquisite woman in all his life.

She said to the intercessor, "I love you very much. I want to make you my forty-first husband. I am the Queen of Heaven." She said she was a very powerful person, much more powerful than Jezebel. She added that Jezebel was her servant.

Many of us think Jezebel is the one we have to be afraid of. But we don't realize that there is a much more powerful demonic spirit who calls herself the "Queen of Heaven."

She said, "My name is Ashtoreth. I am very powerful and very wealthy. I have a great palace up in the Second Heaven, and I will let you live with me in that palace. You will be very happy and very wealthy. You must tell the man you work with [the man of God who was telling me this story] that he must be my prophet. If he will be my prophet and will prophesy what I want him to prophesy, I will make him the greatest prophet in the world, with great power and authority. All will obey him, and I will give him great authority and great riches."

She then took the intercessor up to her great palace in the second heaven. He saw this great palace; the like of its magnificence is beyond anything man has ever built. She said, "This is my home, and you will be here." It had great columns and pillars, and was beautiful both inside and out. And she said, "You will be my forty-first husband, but you must convince the man you work with that he must also be my follower and prophet."

You may doubt this story, saying it is impossible. But I want to remind you that after fasting, when Jesus was tempted of the devil, the devil took him up into a high mountain, and *"shewed unto him all the kingdoms of the world in a moment of time. And the devil said, 'All this power will I give thee, and the glory of them: for that is delivered unto me; and to whomsoever I will I give it. If thou therefore wilt worship me, all shall be thine.'"* When that failed Satan *"brought him to Jerusalem,[8] and set him on a pinnacle of the temple, and said unto him, If thou be the Son of God, cast thyself down from hence"* (Luke 4:5-7, 9).

---

8   The New Agers call it Astral Travel. It is not to be confused with "translation" such as happened to Philip in Acts 8:9.

The demon then said to the intercessor: "My name is Ashtoreth. I am very powerful. I am the Queen of Heaven. I have all the authority to do anything I want to do." Although we know she may be very powerful, she does not have all the power she professes to have, but she does have a lot.

After she left, the intercessor told the man of God what had happened. These two men knew the only way to fight this terrible demonic attack, which was so strong—coming right from the bowels of Hell itself—was to go into days of fasting and prayer.

After they fasted and prayed for some time, the woman returned and said, "Well, what is your answer? What does your man say?"

The intercessor said, "I cannot have anything to do with you."

She became very angry, and said, "Why are you following that carpenter anyway. What good has that carpenter done for you? You are not rich. You are poor, but I will give you so much." She was referring to Jesus, but she could not speak His name.

The intercessor rebuked the demon, "No, we have nothing to do with you. Be gone in the Name of Jesus!"

She threatened him, "You will be sorry for what you have done!"

Then she turned into a hideous, ugly demon. Her beauty was instantly gone, and she was ugly and horrible, neither woman nor man, just a plain demon that had manifested itself as a beautiful woman.

Intercessors Protect Ministries

I don't know why Ashtoreth did not go to the man of God himself, but she came to his intercessor. Intercessors have to be on the alert these days, because we will be the first to be attacked. When we are attacked, those we are interceding for could fall. For every ministry, God has raised up people that are to stand behind them as intercessors, like Aaron and Hur held up the hands of Moses when the Israelites were fighting against the Amalekites. You and I need to have intercessors.

A ministry that does not have intercessors behind it cannot stand very long. They will soon collapse and fall. Those ministries which blossom with people who adulate them, adore them, follow them from place to place, wanting to see the signs, wonders and miracles—but do not pray, travail and fast for them, will fall. These ministries need those who will not only cry for them with tears, but will also fast faithfully for them once a week or at least one day a month.

I believe the secret of my ministry is not that I have great talents, giftings and callings, but that God has raised up intercessors for me as I have served Him in the nations of the world. I have had intercessors back home who could not sleep because the Holy Spirit told them, "Sister Gwen is going through some trial or test." They would be praying and travailing, and knowing things in the Spirit sometimes before I, myself, knew what danger I was in. So I thank God for my intercessors.

Remember what Satan said to Jesus: If you will worship me, I will give you all power over the world. Satan wants to bribe us with the treasures of this world, and blind us to the true pleasures and treasures that are the ones invisible to our eyes.

Remember how Ashtoreth said "Why are you following that carpenter anyway. What good has that carpenter done for you?" God wants to know if you will follow Him because you love Him and not for what you are going to get because you make some sacrifices. Do you love Him enough to follow Him when you don't see what the future holds? Or do you follow Jesus because you hope that some day you will wear a diamond crown? God has to test your love for Him before he can trust you with greatness. He put Abraham through extreme testing when He asked him to sacrifice his son, Isaac. It was only after Abraham was totally obedient to God, that He said that He could bless him and the nations of the world through his descendants. (Genesis 22:16-18)

It is true we do not always see the benefits of the sacrifices we are making in serving the Lord. Ashteroth's great promises of instant gratification blind the soul to the cost that she will demand in exchange for them, but God wants to know if you will follow him when you don't see any rewards this *N. B.* side of Heaven.

I meditated on this revelation, and realized that there has been no ministry that has not been under attack lately by this Queen of Heaven, this Ashtoreth, who has appeared both as a handsome man or a beautiful woman. I meditated, but I didn't talk about it.

Chapter 3

The Seductive Power of Ashtoreth

Roger Sprinkle, who lives in Arkansas, was conscripted into the Vietnam War when he was 18 years old. After a brief training time in the USA, he was given three stripes, making him a sergeant, and shipped overseas. He was put in charge of a platoon of eight men who would fight dangerous jungle warfare against the Vietcong, in a deadly war that was never officially called a war. Many of our finest young men lost their lives during those terrible years. Roger personally told us that the statistics for staying alive in a firefight averaged four minutes eight seconds for a sergeant, three minutes two seconds for a lieutenant, and two minutes four seconds for a captain.

Roger received many decorations for honour and bravery, as well as two purple hearts for being wounded in battle. The third one, he refused. He believes that the reason he came through it alive, though wounded, was because of the faithful prayers of his family back home. The sad fact is that there were 58,209 killed, 153,303 wounded (many are still lying, forgotten in Veterans Hospitals), and almost 1400 missing in action.[9]

Roger told me about his face-to-face encounter with Ashtoreth. He was raised a God fearing Christian, and was close to the Lord when he arrived in Vietnam. However, the experiences he had been through: the killing, the shedding of blood, as well as carelessness in his personal life with God, and committing sins during his brief times of R&R (Rest and Recuperation) in Saigon, caused him to lose the sense of the Presence of God when he was in the thick of the battle. As a result, he was not "dwelling in the secret place of the Most High." This made him vulnerable to satanic attack. Still, he told me, there came a time of extreme danger, when the devil had set up a trap to seduce and ensnare his life and his eternal soul, but God was with him to protect him.

One day when Roger and his men were on patrol, his radioman got a call from their higher command with orders to clear out a village that was about 200 yards ahead of them. He ordered his men to take their positions. As he stepped out of the jungle, he felt as if there was a dome all over the area—a covering about twenty acres in size. He could almost hear the demons playing music—demonic music inside this

---

9   www.history.navy.mil/library/online/american war casualty.htm#t7

dome.[10] He didn't know anything about demons at that time. He didn't know how to do warfare against them. He had a feeling of great danger. He was torn up inside because he loved his men, they had been through many hard times together. But he was under orders, and there was nothing to do but send his men into the village, in spite of what he felt, with the warning, "Watch it!" The village seemed to be empty of all its inhabitants.

He gave the orders to search the village and stood watching to see what would happen. The soldiers went from hut to hut, but he noticed that each time they went into the fourth hut, they came out acting strangely. So he decided to check it out. With his radioman behind him, he stepped into the fourth hut.

In his days of fighting, he had seen many booby traps, some of the scariest and ugliest—you name it! But the booby trap that met his eyes this time in the centre of the hut was nothing like the others! There, in front of him, stood the most gorgeous Vietnamese girl he had ever laid his eyes on. He had seen some pretty girls, but none like this one. She was wearing a beautiful Vietnamese dress, a tunic that went right down to the floor, and it was so lovely she could have

10 To understand more about this demonic canopy read: "How Satan Establishes his Territory in my book: *Redeeming the Land*. See book ads, page 127.

been married in it. They were out in the villages where the people were poor—the girls didn't dress like that out there.

In his testimony at our Youth Camp, Roger told us:

"I started walking around her and I looked her up and down. Now this wouldn't have worked any other time, if it had just been me. I wasn't looking for a woman—I wasn't seeing a woman—that girl—this time. But I looked her up and down, I covered every inch of her and I circled her. And my radioman is standing just inside the door to the right, he got his back out of the door and was standing there. I circled her and I stepped right up, toe to toe—my boots was—I did not touch her—nowhere—not even her dress. I didn't touch her but we was so close. She was looking down at the ground and I looked down on her, she was shorter than I was and I was looking kinda down at her forehead and she was looking down.

"Now she somehow had got the heavens sealed off, and I knew I wasn't getting out of there that day, and I knew I wasn't gonna pray nothing through, but I had been alerted and God had walked me in there. She had sealed the heavens off but I circled her and I sealed her in!

"I stood toe to toe with her and it seemed like forever, but it probably wasn't that long, 'til finally she looked up and she kept raising her head up and she looked right straight in my face. And I was looking right into her eyes and I seen the most hate—and believe me I knew how to hate—but I seen the most hate I've ever seen in my life—I've never seen it since. She could have cut my throat and laughed at me dying!

"I stood there and I looked into her eyes, but I noticed on her dress she had two dragons one on each side, one was looking this way and the other this way [looking in opposite directions] but their heads were turned toward me .... I kept looking in her eyes, and finally her countenance toward me settled enough, that I could see right into the pupil of her eyes, and I noticed that there were two wolves—grown wolves—were in her pupils and they were standing facing each other, this way. They were standing there calm but I had a peace.

"Now, I knew nothing about demons, I don't know if I'd ever heard the word before, but I had such a peace. But when it come to that point, there was like—now it wasn't no big charge—there was like something just went in through my back, just calmly in my back and I went from a peace to a calm. Just totally calm and when I did those wolves began to dance—just back and forth like that—and they were looking at me and they would begin to dance and I was just so calm. And finally, that calmness, they just couldn't come against me! They just went back into her head, just sunk back and I don't know where they went, they just sunk back in her head.

"And she smiled at me with the most beautiful smile you've ever seen and her whole countenance changed. Everything changed about her and something told me, something spoke to me, not a voice, something on my shoulder said: 'She would marry you if you would just ask her.'

"But my time was up, it was time for me to go, what God had accomplished; he was through there. I turned, I walked out the door, my radioman stepped out in front of me, side by side. That [voice] kept telling me: 'You are a fool! I'd go back there and I'd meet that girl'. I kept walking. Now I was tempted, I'm not kidding you, I was tempted—but I kept walking. My men had rushed to the other end of the village, they was already at the jungle. I walked up to them, we passed through that jungle, our choppers was comin' in. It wasn't long 'til our choppers come in, we loaded up and we was out of there.

"I never seen her again, I have never seen her again, she never come to me in my dreams, no way. You know that was never discussed. Usually my men, if I talked to a girl: 'Sarge, what'd she say—more or less—has she got a sister?' You know that was my men, you know that was us. My radioman never mentioned it; my men never talked about it."[11]

Roger knew God had saved him from something terrible. He had run into something incredibly dangerous, more threatening than a bunch of snakes, but he hadn't understood that he was actually looking at a demon manifesting itself into a beautiful woman, who had enough physical and sexual attraction to seduce an army of men.

And then, Roger shared something I had never heard in my life. "A man told me the other day, that a minister said that 'Jesus has a bride—well, Satan

---

11   Roger's testimony is available on CD or DVD. See ads page 125.

Ashtoreth: Goddess of ~~Love~~ Lust

has a bride.' I believe he is right, and I believe I met her." I have since found out that the ultimate goal of those in high witchcraft is to be the bride of Satan.

Ashtoreth was tempting him, and she would have destroyed him in a moment through the spirit of lust.

We are living in momentous days and momentous times, in which God is speaking by His Spirit in a new way. He is revealing truths hidden from us for many generations. Roger's testimony of that beautiful woman, who appeared to him in the little village that had been totally deserted by its inhabitants, is proof of the evil times we are now living in. We know that she would have left with the other people of the village if she had been a normal human being. The fact that she "stayed behind" reveals that she was no ordinary mortal. She was sent by Hell to be there for a purpose, and that was to destroy his soul.

Chapter 4
Ashtoreth: The Destroyer of Lives

Satan wants to destroy the souls of men and women for whom God has a very special destiny. Many pastors, ministers, and evangelists are losing their families, marriages, and ministries through sexual sins. It has happened to too many lives—not only in the religious world, but also in the lives of people playing a leading role in governmental affairs. More and more leading government officials are experiencing sexual demonic attacks on their marriages which destroy their honour and credibility.

Satan does not only have an army of demons, he also has humans who are working with him, and making sacrifices to him, to destroy the marriages of Christians (especially those who are in a prominent ministry). These witches and wizards are also working together to influence men and women in government to make bad decisions in line with an evil agenda. This agenda is bent on destroying the holiness of an individual, a family, a community, a nation, and ultimately, would destroy the world.

Satan works through laws, and by-laws, as well as Hell-inspired organizations and the media.

The schools, from kindergarten to college, are infiltrated with atheism and rebellion against God. The disdaining of ignorance has caused people to reach out to the World-Wide Web to satisfy their quest for knowledge. The Internet is required in most schools as a tool for education. This places the vulnerable in the lap of temptation. I am convinced that every time you connect to the Internet there is the potential of acquiring a demon of pornography.[12] For some, it is no problem, for others, it is their destruction.

Ashtoreth is one of Satan's most powerful and useful weapons in the destruction of ministry and governmental leaders, families, communities, nations and the world.

---

12 See Appendix B, page 103.

Chapter 5

Wisdom Cannot Save You From Ashtoreth

The name of Ashtoreth is mentioned many times in the Old Testament. One of the saddest accounts of her power is in the life of King Solomon.

Solomon was conceived after his father, King David, had fasted for seven days (2 Samuel 12:18). Solomon was chosen by God to build the great Temple in Jerusalem which became a wonder of the world.[13] When he went to Gibeon to offer up sacrifices to the Lord, God appeared to him in a dream and said to him, *"Ask what I shall give thee"* (1 Kings 3:5).

We see Solomon's humility when he answered God:

"Thou hast shewed unto thy servant David my father great mercy, according as he walked before thee in truth, and in righteousness, and

---

13   Although not included in the original "Seven Wonders of the Ancient World" the Temple of Solomon was listed as a Wonder of the World in later lists (see: www.creationconcepts.org and www. templeinstitute.org)

in uprightness of heart with thee; and thou hast kept for him this great kindness, that thou hast given him a son to sit on his throne, as it is this day. And now, O Lord my God, thou hast made thy servant king instead of David my father: and I am but a little child: I know not how to go out or come in. And thy servant is in the midst of thy people which thou hast chosen, a great people, that cannot be numbered nor counted for multitude. Give therefore thy servant an understanding heart to judge thy people, that I may discern between good and bad: for who is able to judge this thy so great a people? And the speech pleased the Lord, that Solomon had asked this thing. And God said unto him, Because thou hast asked this thing, and hast not asked for thyself long life; neither hast asked riches for thyself, nor hast asked the life of thine enemies; but hast asked for thyself understanding to discern judgment; Behold, I have done according to thy words: lo, I have given thee a wise and an understanding heart; so that there was none like thee before thee, neither after thee shall any arise like unto thee. And I have also given thee that which thou hast not asked, both riches, and honour: so that there shall not be any among the kings like unto thee all thy days. And if thou wilt walk in my ways, to keep my statutes and my commandments, as thy father David did walk, then I will lengthen thy days" (1 Kings 3:6-14).

Solomon became one of the greatest kings who ever lived—a man of peace. There were no wars during the time of his 40-year reign. Everything was orderly, and Israel became a land of plenty. The Bible says:

"And God gave Solomon wisdom and understanding exceeding much, and largeness of heart, even as the sand that is on the sea shore. And Solomon's wisdom excelled the wisdom of all the children of the east country, and all the wisdom of Egypt. For he was wiser than all men; than Ethan the Ezrahite, and Heman, and Chalcol, and Darda, the sons of Mahol: and his fame was in all nations round about. And he spake three thousand proverbs: and his songs were a thousand and five. And he spake of trees, from the cedar tree that is in Lebanon even unto the hyssop that springeth out of the wall: he spake also of beasts, and of fowl, and of creeping things, and of fishes. And there came of all people to hear the wisdom of Solomon, from all kings of the earth, which had heard of his wisdom" (1 Kings 4:29-34).

Of all the wisest men of the world, none were wiser than Solomon. The Bible tells us that God gave him the wisdom of all the wise men that were ever before him, and there were great wise men that lived thousands of years ago. Solomon had the wisdom of men like Shem who lived 900 years; so much wisdom did Solomon have. Yet my Bible records:

> *"And he had seven hundred wives, princesses, and three hundred concubines, and his wives turned away his heart. For it came to pass, when Solomon was old, that his wives turned away his heart after other gods, and his heart was not perfect with the Lord his God as was the heart of David his father. For Solomon went after Ashtoreth the goddess of the Zidonians, and after Milcom the abomination of the Ammonites. And Solomon did evil in the sight of the Lord, and went not fully after the Lord, as did David his father. Then did Solomon build an high place for Chemosh, the abomination of Moab, in the hill that is before Jerusalem, and for Molech, the abomination of the children of Ammon. And likewise did he for all his strange wives, which burnt incense and sacrificed unto their gods* (1 Kings 11:3-8).

He was seduced by this powerful demon Ashtoreth who can manifest itself in many forms. I don't need to call it she, it is a he as well. It is a he/she thing. It manifests itself according to the situation. In this case, Solomon became so possessed that he broke his covenant with God. This man of wisdom fell, whom you would think would be the last to fall; it is proof that wisdom is not enough to protect you from Ashtoreth.[14] Even godly preachers, men in high places, who know the Word of God from cover to cover, Genesis to Revelation, are falling. Solomon certainly did. He wrote two thousand hymns, beautiful songs of worship. We have one, the Song of Solomon. That is all we have. Even in that, you can see what is nipping at his heels.

Beloved, why are ministries falling? Why are godly men and women in high places coming down overnight? It isn't the money. It isn't the fame that is bringing them down. It is a spirit of lust.

If you could smell it, you would smell the stench of Hell. But it is perfumed like the perfumes of France. Look at some of the names of the costly perfumes! What does the name of Poison mean? It means "poison!" I would never want to spray poison all over me! I would have to be crazy to put poison all over me. Be careful, girls, what you buy when you go buying your perfume. Some perfume ingredients are known to stimulate sexual desire, and are included to do just that. Don't buy damnation and spray yourself with it. It is better we just use some good old soap and water.

---

14 It is interesting to note that the first false deity that Solomon worshipped was Ashtoreth. One might conclude that his inclination to surround himself with so many wives and concubines would indicate that he was already possessed by the spirit of lust, and that eventually gave way to his worship of that deity in his later years.

I can't stand men who are all perfumed. We need to search out what we are doing these days to ourselves and be careful that we don't spray ourselves with the stench of Hell. Sometimes we can have things in our houses that are poison without the name of poison being on it. Be careful what you do. Be careful how you dress. Be careful what you wear. Be careful what you listen to, be careful what you watch, and choose your friends wisely. Remember the word of God says: *"Blessed is the man that walketh not in the counsel of the ungodly, nor standeth in the way of sinners, nor sitteth in the seat of the scornful"* (Psalm 1:1).

When I look at Solomon, I say, "Solomon, what a fool you were! What a fool you were! These women turned your heart away from God." That is the work of Ashtoreth—to turn the hearts of the people away from God.

When I watch what Ashtoreth has done and I see how she has destroyed so many recently; it grieves my soul. Some of the world's greatest preachers who have impacted the whole world have fallen. I know God has forgiven them, but they can never get back to the ministry they once had. We can forgive them, the Church probably won't. You and I do, we know we are dust. We could fall tomorrow. But they will never regain the honour they once had, and the world will mock them when they weep, and confess, "I have sinned!" Cruel people will walk on them. Even many in the Church will walk on them.

Chapter 6

Physical Strength Cannot Save You From Ashtoreth

Samson's life is recorded in the book of the Judges of Israel, chapters 13-16. He was a Danite. His mother was barren until the Angel of the Lord appeared unto her and told her she would conceive a son, and gave her instructions on her diet, how to raise her son, and the manner of life he had to live. It was called the life of a Nazarite—a life separated unto God, and totally dedicated to God's calling in his life. The token of their covenant as a Nazarite was that they (man or woman) could not cut their hair. Sometimes it was for a lifetime, and sometimes for a certain period of time. It was a life of sacrifice unto God.

Samson was endowed with supernatural strength by the Spirit of the Lord, and could do things which no mortal man had ever done. His exploits are recorded in the story of his life. He obtained the office of a "Judge," i.e. he was a ruler over Israel for twenty years.

He could have lived longer, but he started flirting with sin. First, he married a woman who was not of the tribes of Israel, but an idolatrous Philistine woman. That ended in disaster. Then he visited Gaza and spent half the night with a harlot. In spite of all these things, he still had not lost his power. He thought he could have the best of both things—the sin of the world, and God's gift of power.

But he went one step too far—he fell under the control of Ashtoreth—only, her name was Delilah. The Bible says, *"And it came to pass afterward, that he loved a woman in the valley of Sorek, whose name was Delilah"* (Judges 16:4). This was not a love-match made in Heaven, but came from the very throne of Satan. Satan put his best demon of lust on the assignment of bringing Samson down, and destroying him. The Philistine leaders bribed Delilah, by putting eleven hundred pieces of silver in her hand. It was while Samson was intoxicated by the demonic spirit of lust, that he told her the secrets of his heart, which God had told him never to reveal to anyone. Instantly, he lost it all! One moment of ecstasy cost him his anointing and everything that was precious in his life. Delilah was not a lover, she was an agent from Hell—a beautiful woman, Ashtoreth's servant, who captured the heart of the most anointed, strongest man in the world, and destroyed him as he lay sleeping after a night of passion (Judges 16:15-21).

As I have been meditating again on this story for this book, I thought of the strange paradox—Samson not only lost his strength, he lost his honour, his high position as the Judge of Israel, but also lost his sight, for the Philistines put out his eyes, and bound him with fetters of brass, and put him in the prison to grind the grain—doing the work of a donkey, going around and around. He went from the highest possible position in Israel to serve his enemies, doing the work of a lowly animal, sightless and going in circles, to make their bread.

Today we have men who, because of the aphrodisiac they have taken to enhance their sex-drive, have become blind,[15] lost their honour, their calling—and are prisoners of Satan.

Precious child of God, guard your soul! You don't need to put powder in the wine or the whisky, all you have to do is look once too often. You have to be careful what movies you watch. You have to be careful what books and articles you read. You have to be careful what you tune into on your radio, and demons you connect with on your computer.

We are going to have to start to be our own instructors. There is no one out there who is going to instruct us. The preachers themselves are falling. I once heard a report that when a great gathering

---

15   CBS Evening News 05/26/2005: hhtp://www.cbsnews.com/ stories/2005/05/26/eveningnews/main698124.shtml

was held in Washington D.C. to pray for our country, many of the leaders who came were in their hotel rooms the night before watching pornographic movies. Hotels will tell you that their biggest sell on x-rated movies is when they have preachers' conventions, and the preacher's wives are at home. Sin has crept into our pulpits. So how are we going to preach against it, lest we convict ourselves?[16]

I will never forget that woman who used to call me and weep because of her husband. She would not tell me her name. She asked me to pray for her and said, "Sister Gwen, pray for my husband who is an evangelist. He has women all over this country. I can't tell you my name. I don't want to destroy my husband, but he has women all over. These women would die for him; they are so in love with him." He was a popular evangelist, but he was possessed by the spirit of Ashtoreth.

I have seen great men of God fall. I have seen great women of God fall. Some have been able to climb back again. But most of them will never regain what they lost for "a mess of pottage."

---

16 See Appendix B, page 103.

Chapter 7

Past Victories Cannot Save You From Ashtoreth

At the time of year when "kings go forth to battle," King David sent his men out to fight while he stayed in Jerusalem. He was a soldier who loved a battle, but this time he decided to take a vacation, and let his brave men do the fighting. Soldiers can never retire, unless they are commanded to do so by the Lord, the Commander-in-Chief of the Heavenly Armed Forces, or for physical reasons.

During this time in Jerusalem, David let his guard down. He not only relaxed physically, he relaxed spiritually; it was simple for the devil to trip him up, for he was not on guard for his soul. This made him an easy prey of the enemy.

"One late afternoon, David got up from taking his nap and was strolling on the roof of the palace. From his vantage point on the roof he saw a woman bathing. The woman was stunningly beautiful. David sent to ask about her, and was told, 'Isn't this Bathsheba, daughter of Eliam and wife of Uriah

the Hittite?' David sent his agents to get her. After she arrived, he went to bed with her. (This occurred during the time of 'purification' following her period.) Then she returned home. Before long she realized she was pregnant.

"Later she sent word to David: 'I'm pregnant.'" (2 Samuel 11:2-5; *The Message Bible*)

Ashtoreth had successfully accomplished her mission. Her devilish task was over. But David was in trouble. So he worked out a scheme to hide his sin, but God didn't let him get away with it! Then he had to plan another cover-up! It is true: we cover one sin with another sin.

A second ruling demonic spirit, the demon of murder, then stepped into the picture as part of the devil's plans, which were to ruin David. He sent Uriah back to the battle with sealed orders to give to Joab; orders to station Uriah in the front lines where the fighting was fiercest, then pull back and leave him exposed, so that he was sure to be killed. The orders were carried out and Uriah was killed in the battle (2 Samuel 11:14-17).

David wasn't even convicted of his wicked sins until God sent the Prophet Nathan to him. Nathan told David that he had not only committed adultery, but he had killed Bathsheba's husband with an Ammonite sword (2 Samuel 12:9).

If there is a ministry, calling, or gift which Satan hates and is jealous of, it is the gift of music, after all, he had led the Music and Worship of Heaven. Worship leaders, who are able to bring others into the anointed presence of God, are in danger of Satan's powerful all-out attacks. David, the Sweet Psalmist of Israel, fell to a beautiful woman because he looked too long[17] and Ashtoreth was there, fanning the red hot flames of passion.

She watches every platform when an anointed singer or musician starts to lead God's people in worship, or bring them into the Presence of God through the gift of music. She schemes to bring them down. If David could fall—anyone can! 1 Corinthians 10:12 warns us: *"Wherefore let him that thinketh he standeth take heed lest he fall."*

---

17 See Appendix B, page 103.

Chapter 8
Who Is Ashtoreth?

Who is this Ashtoreth? As I mentioned earlier, The Queen of Heaven is not Mary, the mother of Jesus. Mary does not call herself by that title. Mary, herself announced, *"My soul doth magnify the Lord, and my spirit hath rejoiced in God my Saviour"* (Luke 1:46-47). Mary herself declared her need of a Saviour.

So just WHO is Ashtoreth? As I said earlier in chapter one, Brother Pittman saw five orders of demons, ranked according to their importance in the end-times. Ashtoreth certainly operates at high levels and is, I believe, the highest demon of lust in Satan's army.

Ashtoreth is the Hebrew name for Astarte (Astart, Ashtart, Ashtarte), the chief goddess of the Zidonians who were Phoenicians and Canaanites. She was the goddess of love, fertility, beauty and sexuality. In order to show God's disapproval of idolatrous worship, the Hebrews altered the name of the goddess Astarte, by adding the word *boshet* (shame) to her name thus changing it to Ashtoreth.[18]

---

18   *Encyclopædia Judaica,* Volume 3, page 738.

She was the consort of Baal Baal (Lord Master). Their names are often mentioned together e.g. 1 Samuel 7:4 *"Then the children of Israel did put away Baalim and Ashtaroth, and served the Lord God only."* Various commentaries and Bible Dictionaries agree that Ashtaroth is the plural of Ashtoreth.

Ashtoreth had different names in different cultures, but was one and the same demon. By the Assyrians and Babylonians she was known as Ishtar, by the Egyptians Isis, by the Phoenicians and Carthaginians Astarte, by the Romans Venus, by the Greeks Aphrodite. In Arabia, she was known as Athtar. Another name by which she was known was Asherah, sometimes called "the lady who treads upon the sea."[19] The name Asherah also became synonymous with the wooden objects, poles or idols used in her worship.[20] The Hebrew word Asherah is translated "groves" in the King James Version of the Bible.

In the book of Esther, Hadassah's name meant myrtle. When she was taken into the custody of Hegai, the Keeper of the Women, to prepare her for presentation to the King, she was introduced by her Persian name "Esther." The name Esther which means "star," comes from Ishtar and Astart.[21]

---

19 See Appendix A.
20 *Encyclopædia Judaica,* Vol. 3, page 703-704.
    Fausset's Bible Dictionary.
    www.bible-history.com/faussets/A/Ashtoreth.
21   www.vbm-torah.org/purim/pur-es.htm

Ishtar was associated with the Morning and Evening Star, which we know to be Venus, her Roman name. A star in a circle was one of her symbols, showing her connection to witchcraft and Freemasonry.

According to some ancient writers, Ashtoreth was also known as the goddess of the moon. Baal was also known as the moon god, often represented by a bull or a calf whose horns illustrate the shape of the crescent.[22] It is noteworthy that the star and crescent moon have been shown together in symbol form in the Middle East as far west as Carthage (in modern- day Tunisia) for millenia.[23]

Knowing Islam is ruling in this region, it is not surprising that Ashtoreth, the spirit of lust, occupies the attention of its adherents. From ancient times we can see that Ashtoreth wove and continues to weave her web of lust and destruction amongst the peoples of the earth.

Jeremiah calls her "The Queen of Heaven" and she was worshipped as the highest of all the goddesses. Jeremiah went to the Jews of Egypt with a strong word of rebuke from God regarding their worship of foreign gods but their response was:

"But we will certainly do whatsoever thing goeth forth out of our own mouth, to burn incense

---

22   The equivalent Arabic moon deity was named Sin, from which comes the name Sinai and the Wilderness of Sin mentioned in Exodus 17.
23   http://amos37.com/2009/11/13/hilal-means-crescent/

unto the queen of heaven, and to pour out drink offerings unto her, as we have done, we, and our fathers, our kings, and our princes, in the cities of Judah, and in the streets of Jerusalem: for then had we plenty of victuals, and were well, and saw no evil. But since we left off to burn incense to the queen of heaven, and to pour out drink offerings unto her, we have wanted all things, and have been consumed by the sword and by the famine" (Jeremiah 44: 17-18).

Ashtoreth had seduced them through their worship of her, into thinking only she could satisfy them!

Temple Worship

"The rainfall of winter and the drought of summer were believed to indicate that Baal had died and there was need for him to be brought to life again by magic rites (weeping for Tammuz, who was a Babylonian deity, was similar. It was believed that human tears could help the god bring back the rains; Ezekiel 8:14).

"The Canaanites believed that the gods could be helped to bring about fertility of the soil if the people fertilized one another in the places of worship. Therefore, there was a crude sexuality in the name of religion. Every Canaanite sanctuary had its own prostitutes for that purpose. Each sanctuary was dominated by a wooden pole, or asherah, which symbolized the female sex principle and the name of the goddess Asherah, and by an erect stone or mazzebah, which symbolized male sexuality.

"The Canaanites believed that the gods could be persuaded, even coerced, by magic ritual. This led to the extreme of child sacrifice. Sanctuaries to the gods were made on artificial mounds or 'high places,' often placed on hilltops in the belief they brought the worshippers physically closer to the gods."[24]

It is certain that the worship of Ashtoreth was connected with the most impure rites, being extremely licentious and abominable.

A Visit to Corinth

In 1998 we took an End-Time Handmaidens and Servants tour to Greece. It was a never-to-be-forgotten experience. I will always remember our visit to Corinth. I had visited the ruins of that old city in 1961, but this time I learned so much more, because we had an official tour guide.

I remember her pointing to the hill rising 1,500 feet above the south side of the city, and looking at the ruins of what had once been the great pagan Temple of Aphrodite (or Ashtoreth). This temple and its 1,000 temple prostitutes (female and male) greatly influenced the city's culture and morals. The morality of a nation is always determined by

---

24   Ralph Gower, *The New Manners and Customs of Bible Times* (Chicago, Moody Press, 1987), page 335. Permission requested.

its spiritual condition. The nation that forgets God becomes immoral and filthy with sin.

When the kings of Judah were holy—the nation was holy; when they were sinful—the nation was corrupted. When Joash became king *"he brake down the houses of the sodomites, that were by the house of the Lord, where the women wove hangings for the grove"* (2 Kings 23:7).

Archeologists have discovered artifacts in northern Sinai dating back from the last quarter of the eighth century BCE, and another site near Hebron. These artifacts have inscriptions which read "to Yahweh and his Asherah." What a depth of depravity the people had sunk to that they "married" Yahweh and Ashtoreth!

These artifacts reveal a deeply rooted Asherah cult, in which both men and women would have participated. In 2 Kings 21:7, the Hebrew says that King Manasseh placed "an image of Asherah" in the Temple. In the subsequently written 2 Chronicles 33:7, he is said to have set up, literally, "an image of the symbol."[25]

The tour guide told us that the honourable ladies of the city never associated with temple prostitutes. To make sure they were separate from the prostitutes (who were the objects of their husband's idolatrous worship), they would do their shopping in the market

25   Miriam Feinberg Vamosh, *Women in the Time of the Bible* (Herzlia, Palphot Ltd. 2007), page 60. www.palphot.com.

when they knew they wouldn't be there. She also said that the temple prostitutes (called priestesses) were beautiful. They posed as models for sculptures. If you visit the Acropolis in Athens, you will see the remains of a great building, which has pillars, called *karyatides,* sculpted in the shape of women. It is quite moving to think you are, most probably, looking at an actual artistic replica of a temple prostitute, who lived over two thousand years ago.

When Paul lived in Corinth, the population was approximately 500,000. It was a naval city, so there were many travellers. Paul lived there with Aquila and Priscilla (Acts 18:1-2) for one year and six months. He had a revival, and founded a church.

According to his letters to the Corinthians he had to deal very strongly with them about moral issues, (1 Corinthians 6:9-20). He lists their former sins, and warns them *"and such were some of you: but ye are washed, but are sanctified, but ye are justified in the name of the Lord Jesus, and by the spirit of God"* (1 Corinthians 6:11).

You can understand why Paul was so reluctant to allow women to minister in the church when some of them had come from a background of pagan temple prostitution.

Knowing that one of Ashteroth's names is Aphrodite, and remembering that there is a plant or substance called an "aphrodisiac" which is used to arouse sexual desire, we can see the connection to pagan temple worship with its many temple prostitutes and sodomites.

We heard plenty of stories about aphrodisiacs in Hong Kong. They were used in the bars when the soldiers would come in on R&R, and a pretty little Chinese "Susie Wong" would sit down on the seat beside him, smile coquettishly, and slip a little powder into his drink. Before he knew it, he was in a state of sexual intoxication that drove him to such madness that he lost his sensibility and sensitivity to what was right and what was wrong; and he found himself seduced physically, mentally and spiritually.

There was hardly a month that went by during the Vietnam War when you wouldn't read of some soldier who had been found dead—together with a prostitute in a cheap hotel room, both overdosed on an aphrodisiac. Their bodies were found in the "embrace of death." Some aphrodisiacs are really dangerous; they have caused permanent, irreversible blindness within 45 minutes of taking them.[26] Some of today's aphrodisiacs are sold under the names Viagra, Cialis and Levitra.

---

26   CBS Evening News 05/26/2005: hhtp://www.cbsnews.com/ stories/2005/05/26/eveningnews/main698124.shtml

The Giants

There is a place of great antiquity mentioned in Genesis 14:5, called "Ashteroth-karnaim," which means: "Ashteroth of the two horns."[27] It is believed the *Rephaim* (giants[28]) originated there. King Og, the giant whose bed was nine cubits long, was king of the city of Ashtaroth, in Bashan, (Deuteronomy 1: 4). It is interesting to note that both these places, with Ashteroth's name on them were dwelling places of giants. So one can assume that the giants were associated with Ashteroth. They were probably related to the sons of Anak, or Anakim that frightened the ten spies into giving the report that the Promised Land couldn't be taken.

Were these the original giants (the Nephilim) who had lived in the time of the flood? I don't think so. Could there have been a taint of their DNA in the bloodline of one of the wives of Noah's three sons? We know that descendents of Ham went to live in that territory, and brought the sins of pagan worship and sexual perversions. In fact, the sin of sodomy is named after Sodom, one of the chief cities of Canaan. There has been a trace of giant races that have come down through the centuries. The original giants were

---

27 Merril F. Unger, *The New Unger's Bible Dictionary* (Chicago, Moody Press, 1988), page 114.
28 *Strong's Exhaustive Concordance*, #7497, Hebrew and Chaldee Dictionary.

destroyed in the great flood, for that was the purpose of the flood, to destroy them.

Some of the Greek and Roman mythology that you have read about in school, dates back to actual accounts of beings who lived at that time, who were part human and part spirit. They had supernatural abilities and they were the offspring that was not of God, but of Satan. It was a satanic combination, a work of Satan to scar the handiwork of God when God created Adam and Eve in His likeness.

My Chinese daughter-in-law, Su, told me that in the area of northwest China where her family originally came from, there is an ancient traditional myth that the gods used to come down to earth and cohabit with women. The children of these unions were half human and half god. They did not get this account from the Bible; this is ancient Chinese history. Chinese history dates hundreds of years earlier than any of our history, including the Bible. But it is not as reliable.

Chapter 9

The Power of Ashtoreth

When Satan told Jesus in Luke 4:6, *"All this power will I give thee, and the glory of them: for that is delivered unto me; and to whomsoever I will I give it,"* he was not lying to Jesus; he knew he could not lie to Him, for he knew Jesus knew truth. Satan still has limited power on the earth. He raises up some, and pulls down others; but not many can stay in power long when they are under his control. There are few men who were greater, more powerful or who had conquered more nations, than Nebuchadnezzar, Alexander the Great, Julius Caesar, Napoleon, Hitler, Stalin, Mao Tse-Tung, etc. but their time of power was very short, compared to the reign of Christ Jesus.

Now who is Ashtoreth? What is Ashtoreth's power? Is it only wealth? No, it is the greatest, strongest, evil power that is in the world—the power of the lust of the flesh. Satan knows that God created us with the ability to reproduce after our own kind. He hates us because of that. But he takes that gift to procreate that God has given us, and he warps it, ruins it, perverts and destroys it. He makes it ugly, and he uses Ashtoreth to deceive many into believing lust is love. He destroys bodies, and breaks hearts. Many ministries have been destroyed by this Ashtoreth demon, who has power not only to *"transform himself into an angel of light"* (2 Corinthians 11:14), but to manifest himself as a woman to seduce men, or as a man to seduce women.

Aimee Semple McPherson

In the early 1900's Aimee Semple McPherson was beautiful, successful and the most powerful woman preacher in the world; thousands attended her services. By 1923 she had built Angelus Temple in Los Angeles. She was lonely and wanted to be loved. In the 1930's along came a singer who said he would support her in her ministry. She fell in love with him and they married, but all was not as it seemed. He was in the spirit of Ashtoreth in male form, as he won her heart, and then turned against her, divorced her and publicly ridiculed her. Although she was broken-hearted, she continued to preach the gospel and bring thousands more souls to Christ.[29]

Kathryn Kuhlman

Kathryn Kuhlman, the preacher with a great anointing for healing between the 1930s and 1970s,

---

29 *Aimee—The Life Story of Aimee Semple McPherson* (Los Angeles, Four Square Publications, 1979).

fell under the power of this Ashtoreth spirit but was able to climb back and become greater than when she fell. An evangelist came to the city where she was preaching. He was handsome. They fell in love. The only trouble was, he had a wife. He divorced his wife and married Kathryn Kuhlman, and her ministry collapsed. One day she came to the end of herself. She called it "dead-end street." She said, "Where do I go from here, My God?" God said, "You have to give him up if you ever want me to use you again." And she did. I don't say she stopped loving him, only the heart can do that. But she said goodbye, and walked a lonely life from there on out, but fulfilled the call of God on her life.[30] I had the privilege of meeting her in Macau; we stayed in the same hotel. She was sold out to God.

Ashtoreth Cannot Give You What God Can

Ashtoreth cannot give you what God can. Ashtoreth is a thief who will rob you of everything God wants to give to you. She will bid the highest price for your soul. I have seen young people start out with the call of God, the anointing, the gifts of God and the Holy Spirit in their lives. You see they have the potential of making a mark in the Church of the Living God. Then Ashtoreth comes along, leaving broken hearts and broken churches. Church

---

30   www.healingandrevival.com
     Jamie Buckingham, *Daughter of Destiny* (Alachua, Bridge-Logos Foundation, 1999).

after church is falling apart. Ministries are falling apart. Families are falling apart. Lives are falling apart. Denominations are falling apart. Some of those chosen vessels manage to make it back to God, but they leave a trail of broken hearts and confused lives behind them. That's Ashtoreth!

We must never underestimate Lucifer's evil intentions. Remember what he did when he was the leading worshipper in Heaven! Isaiah, writing by revelation, gives us the account of Satan's rebellion against Almighty God: *"For thou hast said in thine heart, I will ascend into heaven, I will exalt my throne above the stars of God: I will sit also upon the mount of the congregation, in the sides of the north: I will ascend above the heights of the clouds; I will be like the most High"* (Isaiah 14:13-14).

If Satan dared to seize the Throne of God, there are no limits to what he will try to do or whom he will try to destroy. He certainly attempted to destroy Jesus' mission in life when he tempted him three times in the wilderness.

One of Satan's most powerful and useful weapons in the destruction of ministry leaders' souls is Ashtoreth. She serves him faithfully, and has caused many great men and women to fall.

Some ministers have, at one time, been an example of holiness; they have been admired, idolized, have had world-renowned television programmes, and gained multitudes of followers. Of money they have had no lack; they may have lived in multi-million dollar houses, have had huge bank accounts, diamond rings to dazzle your eyes. For some of these ministers, the spirit of lust has accompanied this success and has driven them to lust after food, clothes, power, wealth, possessions, fame, and popularity, bringing about their downfall. Some are also led on into drugs, alcohol, and insatiable desires for all kinds of sexual acts, including perversions, pædophilia,[31] masturbation,[32] and sodomy. That's Ashtoreth!

She has shaken kingdoms throughout the ages of time. These evil sins have destroyed great men and women, cities, kingdoms and nations.

What Will Destroy A Nation?

Two of the main things that will destroy a nation are:

1. How a Nation Treats Israel:

God promised Abraham in Genesis 12:2-3: *"I will make of thee a great nation, and I will bless thee, and make thy name great; and thou shalt be a blessing: and I will bless them that bless thee, and curse him*

---

31   Sexual feelings directed towards children.
http://oxforddictionaries.com/definition/pædophilia

32   Masturbation: "to manipulate one's own genitals, or the genitals (of another) for sexual gratification" *Websters New World Dictionary of the American Language*: 1980 Shuster and Shuster: (Published by The World Publishing Company) See Appendix C, page 106.

that curseth thee: and in thee shall all families of the earth be blessed." The nation that fights and opposes Israel or the Jew will be cursed. Look what happened to Rome after 70 AD, Russia after the *Pogroms*,[33] Nazi Germany after the murder of six million Jews, and even Great Britain, when they took the side of the Arabs and refused to allow the Jews to return to their homeland, but imprisoned them in Cyprus. England lost her great Empire.

I know God has blessed the End-Time Handmaidens Ministry since we started blessing Israel, and standing with her and for her.

2. The Loss of Good Moral Codes in a Nation:

When a nation falls into gross sin, *"Ichabod"* (the Glory of God has departed, 1 Samuel 4:21) is written over it. The morals of our nations have declined to such a degree that God has had to lift off His mantle of blessing.

When God promised to give Abraham the land of the Canaanites he said: *"In the fourth generation they shall come hither again: for the iniquity of the Amorites is not yet full"* (Genesis 15:16). God knew exactly how long it would take before the Day of Judgment for that land. When the Amorites' cup of

---

33 Pogrom: an organized massacre of a particular ethnic group, in particular that of Jews in Russia or eastern Europe.
    http://oxforddictionaries.com/definition/pogrom

iniquity was full, God raised up Moses to lead His people to the Promised Land.

Our churches are no longer aflame with righteousness. In the 1800's America was visited by a renowned French author, historian, and philosopher, Alexis de Tocqueville. He was tremendously impressed and wrote four volumes entitled *Democracy in America.* The following quote is often attributed to him: "I sought for the greatness and genius of America in her commodious harbors and her ample rivers—and it was not there; in her fertile fields and boundless forests—and it was not there; in her rich mines and her vast world commerce—and it was not there; in her democratic Congress and her matchless Constitution—and it was not there. Not until I went into the churches of America, and heard her pulpits AFLAME WITH RIGHTEOUSNESS, did I understand the secret of her genius and power. America is great because America is good, and if America ever ceases to be good, America will cease to be great."[34]

---

34 www.bibleweb.com/2006/12/de-tocqueville-america-is-great-because.htm

Chapter 10

Ashtoreth Destroys the King's Daughter and Sons

There was a beautiful woman in the Bible. Her name was Tamar. She was a king's daughter. I am going to tell you her story. It is very blunt. But the Bible puts it bluntly. I am quoting from *The Message Bible*. 2 Samuel 13:1-19:

"Sometime later this happened: Absalom, David's son, had a sister who was very attractive. Her name was Tamar. Amnon, also David's son [his firstborn], was in love with her. Amnon was obsessed with his sister Tamar to the point of making himself sick over her. She was a virgin, so he couldn't see how he could get his hands on her. Amnon had a good friend, Jonadab, the son of David's brother, Shimeah. Jonadab was exceptionally streetwise. He said to Amnon, "Why are you moping around like this day after day—you, the son of the king. Tell me, what's eating at you?

"In a word, Tamar," said Amnon. *"My brother Absalom's sister. I am in love with her."* [They had the same father but not the same mother because David had several wives.]

"Here's what you do," said Jonadab. *"Go to bed and pretend you're sick. When your father comes to visit you, say, 'Have my sister Tamar come and prepare some supper for me here where I can watch her and she can feed me.'"*

So Amnon took to his bed and acted sick. And when the king came to visit, Amnon said, "Would you do me a favor? Have my sister Tamar come and make some nourishing dumplings here where I can watch her and be fed by her?"

David sent word to Tamar who was home at the time. "Go to the house of your brother Amnon and prepare a meal for him." [Sounds innocent, doesn't it!]

So Tamar went to her brother Amnon's house. She took dough, kneaded it, formed it into dumplings and cooked them while he watched from his bed. [I will tell you how they cooked them, because I have been looking into the Mishneh about this. She rolled this dough into little round balls and dropped them into the water, boiled them, then took them out and fried them in olive oil. Sounds tasty.] *But when* she took the cooking pot and served him, he wouldn't eat.

Amnon said, *"Clear everyone out of the house."* And they all cleared out. [She should have been suspicious by then. But she was naïve.] *Then he said to Tamar, "Bring the food into my bedroom, where we can eat in privacy."* [With no one in the house they were already in privacy.] *She took the nourishing dumplings she had prepared and brought them to her brother Amnon in his bedroom. But when she got ready to feed him, he grabbed her and said, "Come to bed with me, sister!"*

"No, brother!" she said, "Don't hurt me! This kind of thing isn't done in Israel! Don't do this terrible thing! Where could I ever show my face? And you—you'll be out on the street in disgrace. Oh, please! Speak to the king—he'll let you marry me."

But he wouldn't listen. Being much stronger than she, he raped her.

No sooner had Amnon raped her than he hated her—an immense hatred. The hatred that he felt for her was greater than the love he'd had for her. "Get up," he said, "and get out!"

"Oh no, brother," she said. "Please! This is an even worse evil than what you just did to me."

But he wouldn't listen to her. He called for his valet. "Get rid of this woman. Get her out of my sight! And lock the door behind her!" The valet threw her out and locked the door behind her.

She was wearing a long-sleeved gown. (That's how early virgin princesses used to dress from early adolescence on.) Tamar poured ashes on her head, then she ripped the long-sleeved gown, held her head in her hands, and walked away, sobbing as she went.

Her brother Absalom said to her, "Has your brother Amnon had his way with you?"'

I want to stop right there in the story to bring out a truth. Amnon's name in the original Hebrew means "faithful, true, worthy of trust." Here in verse 20, when Absalom speaks Amnon's name, he adds, right in the middle of it, the letter *"yod,"* which changes it to "Aminon," an expression of contempt[35] for his half brother who had become a thief, one who steals what does not belong to him.

When you men steal a girl's virginity you rob her of her highest treasure.[36] And when you girls readily give your virginity to a man, you're giving him something that will make him hate you and despise you. He may marry you, but he will never trust you. The rest of his life he will always be jealous and

---

35 James Hastings M.A., D.D., editor, *A Dictionary of the Bible, Volume 1* (Peabody, Hendrickson Publishers, 1988), 83.

36 See Appendix C, page 106.

suspicious that you would do the same thing with somebody else.

And now, in verse 20, we hear the good side of Absalom. *"'Now, my dear sister, Let's keep it quiet—a family matter. He is after all your brother. Don't take this so hard.' Tamar lived in her brother Absalom's home, bitter and desolate."* Her life was ruined. Not only was *her* life ruined, Absalom's life was ruined because he took on himself the spirit of his sister's offense, and began hating his brother and planning his murder. So much tragedy for a few minutes of unbridled lust! But that is what Ashtoreth will do with a promising life! Amnon was David's firstborn son. Like Esau, he sold his birthright for a "mess of pottage." It is amazing what great things people will throw away in order to satisfy the spirit of lust.

Why am I telling you this story? This is a story of a young woman with a promising future. She was King David's beautiful daughter, the princess of Israel. She was innocent, obviously, because she was so naïve (like Eve in the Bible), but spent the rest of her life in desolation because she could never marry. They didn't keep it in the family! It wasn't long before Absalom had his own brother Amnon killed, and the blood flowed in the House of David.

How many men have promised some trusting woman, "I will love you forever," and tomorrow they say, "Leave me alone! I never want to see you again!"

And how many girls have come to the men that they love, and said, "Please help me; I am pregnant!" only to be told, "That's your problem. You'd better get an abortion." Or, "I don't believe it is my kid. It is probably someone else's." Broken hearts. Broken pieces. Broken lives are very hard to put back together again. Sometimes, all you can do is patch them up and make the best of it.

Some of you have already gone too far. Some of you already feel ashamed, like Tamar. Your face is red when you see the man that you gave your body to.

Years ago, I remember my husband coming home from work one night and saying, "I worked with a man today who told me he tries to seduce a virgin every day." That was his demonic obsession—to seduce one girl a day. Be wise! I am beseeching you, like a mother in Israel. I am talking to you really plainly. I want to see you in Heaven.

If you have sinned, if you have been seduced, if you have been molested or even raped, keep it in the King's family. Don't go telling the whole world. Don't sell your story to the tabloids! Go to the family of God for prayer and counselling. Make sure, by taking appropriate action, that the person who did this terrible sin is never able to repeat it. And don't forget to tell Jesus and let Him heal you. Let God give you the grace to forgive so that your sins can also be forgiven. And you men, be careful how you handle the daughters of the King—or any other woman.

We are facing hard days ahead. We don't know what the months and years will bring. In spite of all man-made promises, prosperity and peace, things are falling apart more every day in nation after nation. We are physically bankrupt because we are morally bankrupt.

On the other hand, God may have a wonderful surprise for you. If you are contemplating an important life's decision such as marriage, go to the wise women and the wise men, and tell them. Make sure that they all agree and feel it is the right thing you are doing. And if you see a question in their face, and see their eyes are troubled about your decision to marry, stop and think before you make that trip to the altar. Sometimes, they see things in the Spirit that you don't see because you are so much in the flesh—"in love." It is hard to see in the Spirit when you live in the flesh.

Ashtoreth has never been more alive than she is today. And she is waiting for that exact moment in your life when you will be gullible and weak. She is lovely and beautiful, or he will look really handsome. What did Roger do in my earlier story? He walked around, and around, and around, and around. Take a second look before you leap.

There are many Amnons in the world, and there is one waiting for you to make him dumplings. Don't do it! Don't do it! Let him die alone in bed! Don't be seduced by their tears, by their threats to commit suicide—"If you don't love me, I will kill myself!" Don't do it! I have seen them threaten their prey, "I'll kill myself! I'll jump from this window! I will jump off the bridge!" Let them! It is better than you jumping into the fires of Hell!

Don't do it! See Appendix C, page 106.

Chapter 11
Can Ashtoreth Be Overcome?

How can you overcome that spirit of Ashtoreth? Ashtoreth is neither omnipresent nor omniscient. She succeeds at her craft by the use of a network of demons who follow her commands in abject fear. God has not left us without weapons to defeat them.

1. Prayer & Fasting:

Jesus told His disciples that certain demons do not come out without prayer and fasting (Matthew 17:21). What did the intercessor and the man of God do in chapter 2? They started to pray and fast.[37] Fasting is one of the greatest weapons of power against the enemy of our souls. When you are not sure about a relationship, call a fast. Get clear guidance from God. There is something about sex demons, they leave on the third day of fasting because they like to eat, and they especially like meat. That is why the Buddhist monks, who are supposed to live celibate lives, are vegetarians. That is why many saints

---

37   For more teaching on Prayer and Fasting see my books *Pour Out Your Heart* and *Your Appointment with God*. See book ads, page 127.

are vegetarians—because they know they must overcome the flesh.[38] There is something about that meat-eating beast that makes the blood hot. Feed a dog raw meat, and he will become vicious.

The following testimony was sent to us by one of our End-Time Handmaidens:

"*A very* unfortunate and unexpected situation took place in my life in which someone I knew tried to force himself on me. I was not only very upset by this but found that I had to battle a spirit of lust that was trying to make inroads into my life because of his unclean touch. I knew from being in the deliverance ministry in the past that these dark spirits detest being in the light, they like to hide in secrecy, so I decided to go to some friends and explain my problem so that the demon would not gain any power from being hidden. It was embarrassing but I was very honest about the situation. My friends prayed for me, yet I still had the battle and would wake up in the middle of the night with that spirit just waiting for me to let my guard down.

"I was determined to get free—and soon— so I went to my pastor and explained what had

---

38 I am not suggesting that you shouldn't ever eat meat, just follow the leading of the Holy Spirit and don't eat too much of it.

happened and the ensuing results. He knew that I lived a clean life; he had known me for many years. "You are going to have to go on a fast to get free and I suggest an Esther Fast with no food or water for three days. That will break the power of this spirit. The spirit of lust is not only trying to lure you into a life of darkness and secrecy, but it wants to steal your destiny." Then he prayed and anointed me for an Esther Fast.

"A few days later I knew it was time to fast so I stayed quietly with the Lord, worshipping and praying as I fasted, I was desperate! I am so happy to report that at the end of that fast I was totally free!"

2. The Powerful Blood of Jesus:

Revelation 12:9 and 11 says; *"And the great dragon was cast out, that old serpent, called the Devil, and Satan, which deceiveth the whole world: he was cast out into the earth, and his angels were cast out with him ....And they overcame him by the blood of the Lamb, and by the word of their testimony; and they loved not their lives unto the death."*

God's Holy Promise to us is, *"They overcame him **by the Blood of the Lamb**, and by the word of their testimony; and they loved not their lives unto the death."*

Beloved, the Blood will **never** lose its power. The Blood of Jesus is still alive today. Just claim the Blood of Jesus. I do it all the time. Put the Blood of Jesus against the most powerful demon of Hell. He's got to leave.

When you are in a dangerous situation, pray for the Blood of Jesus to cover you and protect you. If the blood of a slain lamb on the door posts of the Israelites, could protect them when the destroyer passed through the land, killing all the first-born of man and beast in Egypt, then surely the Blood of Jesus, which is much more powerful, can protect us from all evil.

3. Read the Word of God

Paul said to Timothy; "*Study to shew thyself approved unto God, a workman that needeth not to be ashamed, rightly dividing the word of truth*" (2 Timothy 2:15).

The Psalmist said in Psalm 119:11, "*Thy word have I hid in mine heart, that I might not sin against thee.*" The entire psalm is dedicated to honouring the word of God. It is part of the armour of God every soldier of the Cross must use—"*the sword of the Spirit, which is the word of God*" (Ephesians 6:17).

When Jesus was tempted of the devil in the wilderness, Jesus defeated him by quoting the Word of God. We would be shocked to know how few of

God's children have ever read God's Word from cover to cover.

4. The Power of the Anointed Life:

Another way is through the Kingly Anointing. The anointing of God will take you a long way. Without the Kingly Anointing you don't stand much chance of overcoming Ashtoreth. 2 Kings 9:1-10 says:

> *"And Elisha the prophet called one of the children of the prophets, and said unto him, Gird up thy loins, and take this box of oil in thine hand, and go to Ramothgilead: And when thou comest thither, look out there Jehu the son of Jehoshaphat the son of Nimshi, and go in, and make him arise up from among his brethren, and carry him to an inner chamber; Then take the box of oil, and pour it on his head, and say, Thus saith the LORD, I have anointed thee king over Israel. Then open the door, and flee, and tarry not. So the young man, even the young man the prophet, went to Ramothgilead. And when he came, behold, the captains of the host were sitting; and he said, I have an errand to thee, O captain. And Jehu said, Unto which of all us? And he said, To thee, O captain. And he arose, and went into the house; and he poured the oil on his head, and said unto him, Thus saith the LORD God of Israel, I have anointed thee king over the people of the LORD, even over*

Israel. And thou shalt smite the house of Ahab thy master, that I may avenge the blood of my servants the prophets, and the blood of all the servants of the LORD, at the hand of Jezebel. For the whole house of Ahab shall perish: and I will cut off from Ahab him that pisseth against the wall, and him that is shut up and left in Israel: And I will make the house of Ahab like the house of Jeroboam the son of Nebat, and like the house of Baasha the son of Ahijah: And the dogs shall eat Jezebel in the portion of Jezreel, and there shall be none to bury her. And he opened the door, and fled."

Jehu received the Kingly Anointing together with prophetic instructions of all he must do, and all that would come to pass. It was in the authority of this anointing upon him that Jehu was able to succeed in his mission to destroy the demonic power that was ruling over Israel.

Before Jehu could get to Ashtoreth, he had to get to one of Ashtoreth's top servants, Jezebel. As I said earlier, in chapter two, Ashtoreth declared Jezebel was her servant. [39] Remember how Jezebel supported and fed four hundred and fifty of Baal's prophets; and four hundred of Ashtoreth's (1 Kings 18:19). Demon spirits often co-operate and work together to do the devil's work.

---

39   Jezebel was the daughter of Ethbaal, King of the Zidonians and Ashtoreth was the chief goddess of the Zidonians (1 Kings 16:31).

When Jezebel heard that Jehu was on his way to Jezreel, she knew he was coming to kill her. She tried the old female tactics of seduction through her beauty—she painted her face and adorned her head and looked out of the window.[40] *"When Jehu came through the city gate, she called down, 'So, how are things, "Zimri," you dashing king-killer?'"*

He did not answer her. You never make conversation with demons. *"Jehu looked up at the window and called, 'Is there anybody up there on my side?' Two or three palace eunuchs looked out. He ordered 'Throw her down! They threw her out the window. Her blood spattered the wall and the horses, and Jehu trampled her under his horse's hooves. Then Jehu went inside and ate his lunch. During lunch he gave orders, 'Take care of that damned woman, give her a decent burial—she is, after all, a king's daughter.' They went out to bury her, but there was nothing left of her but skull, feet, and hands"* (2 Kings 9:32-36 *The Message Bible*). That is the fulfillment of the prophecy that Elijah the Tishbite gave in 1 Kings 21:23.

Don't get into an argument with Jezebel or Ashtoreth. Don't stop to discuss anything! You may be seduced. Jehu did not even look at Jezebel's beautiful face, or her beautiful hair style—with the

---

40   In the *Encyclopædia Judaica,* volume 3, page 738, there is a picture with a caption that reads: "Ivory plaque from Nimrud, Mesopotamia, c. eighth century B.C.E., thought to be a representation of Astarte who, like her temple prostitutes, lured men from her window."

jewellery in it, nor how her eyes were painted. She had seduced thousands of men with her beauty, including Ahab, the crown prince of Israel, whose wife she became.

Never look into the eyes of Jezebel or Ashtoreth. Because when you look into those eyes you will see dancing wolves. Instead, Jehu said, *"'Is there anybody up there on my side?' Two or three palace eunuchs looked out. He ordered, Throw her down!' They threw her out the window."* There is your key! A eunuch is someone who cannot be sexually seduced. A eunuch does not have the same sexual desire as an ordinary person. The Word says that there will be virgins who will have a special place in the Kingdom.

The Apostle John wrote:

*"And I looked, and, lo, a Lamb stood on the mount Sion, and with him an hundred forty and four thousand, having his Father's name written in their foreheads. And I heard a voice from heaven, as the voice of many waters, and as the voice of a great thunder: and I heard the voice of harpers harping with their harps: And they sung as it were a new song before the throne, and before the four beasts, and the elders: and no man could learn that song but the hundred and forty and four thousand, which were redeemed from the earth. These are they which were **not defiled** with women; for they are virgins. These*

*are they which follow the Lamb whithersoever
he goeth. These were redeemed from among
men, being the firstfruits unto God and to the
Lamb. And in their mouth was found no guile:
for they are without fault before the throne of
God"* (Revelation 14:1-5).

Revelation 14:4 describes them; *"These are they
which follow the Lamb whithersoever He goeth."* Be a
follower of the Lamb. Jesus mingled with women. It
is not wrong for a man to talk with a woman. He sent
His disciples off to town and waited for the woman to
come and talk with Him. He knew she was coming.
He had an appointment with her at the well. That
was a holy "date." It was an appointment with God
(John 4:3-30).

In describing this firstfruits company it says in
Revelation, *"These were redeemed from among men
being the firstfruits unto God"* Can you be among the
firstfruits Company?

Do you know what the firstfruits are? The
firstfruits are the first ripenings of grain, the garden,
or the fruit of the orchard. They are picked from the
tree or the garden before the full crop becomes ripe.
Could they be the ones John is referring to when he
says in Revelation 20:6, *"Blessed and holy is he that
hath part in the first resurrection: on such the second
death hath no power, but they shall be priests of God
and of Christ, and shall reign with him a thousand*

years"? Could there be those who will be caught up into Heaven before the general resurrection, or what we call "the rapture" of the bride of Christ? Will there be some souls who will be "raptured" before "the rapture"? The qualifications are high! *"And in their mouth was found no guile, for they are without fault before the Throne of God"* (Revelation 14:5).

The firstfruits of the barley come in at Passover time. The harvest comes in seven weeks later. That means something big could happen any time right now before the Rapture.

5. Live a Holy Life in Obedience to God:

Is it really possible to live a holy life? You must desire to live a holy life. You must desire to be like Jesus. Make Him the Lover of your soul. Fall in love with Jesus. That is what happened to me when I wrote my first book (which we still publish): *Song of Love.*[41]

Don't flirt with Ashtoreth. Don't play with sin. Don't see how far you can go and get away with it. Don't seduce anyone to sin, and don't allow anyone to seduce you. Woman of God, be careful with your eyes! Your eyes can entice men. Let there be nothing but the look of holiness and purity. Woman of God, don't copy the worldly dress, make-up, actions, or flirtatious ways that are unholy. I have seen women

---

41 See book ads, page 126.

in church leadership flirt with Christian men of God. Don't let Ashteroth lead you astray: *"Who can find a virtuous woman? For her price is far above rubies"* (Proverbs 31:10).

Man of God, be careful what you look at and keep looking at: make sure you rein in your thoughts, in accordance with God's Holy Word, and do not lust after a woman. *"Casting down imaginations, and every high thing that exalteth itself against the knowledge of God, and bringing into captivity every thought to the obedience of Christ"* (2 Corinthians 10:5).

Chapter 12

Ashtoreth Can Be Overcome
Joseph, the Overcomer

Joseph grew up in a family where he suffered much rejection. His mother died in childbirth when his younger brother, Benjamin, was born. Joseph was but a young child when this happened. His father, Jacob had two wives and it was Joseph's mother, Rachel who was the love of Jacob's life. His ten sons by his other wife, Leah and his wives' maid servants always resented Joseph because they knew how much his father loved him. Joseph's whole story can be found in Genesis, chapters 37 and 39-48.

When he was only seventeen years old[42] God gave him a dream. He gave him a double-dream. It was this dream that kept him going through the hard times.

His brothers sold him into slavery, and he spent the rest of his life in Egypt. He went from trial to

---

42   Jasher, *The Authentic Annals of the Early Hebrews Also Known as The Book of Jasher* (Kearney, Morris Publishing, 1995), chapter 41:9-14, pages 90-91.

blessing, from blessing to trial and then trial to blessing.

It was when he was holding a position of honour and dignity that Satan tried to seduce him through an Egyptian woman, the wife of his master. She was possessed with the spirit of Ashtoreth. She didn't love Joseph. She wanted his body. She could think of nothing but that young, handsome Hebrew slave. Day after day, she begged him to "sleep" with her. Day after day he refused her, "You're my master's wife. How could I violate his trust and sin against God?"

One day, she grabbed him by the coat, begging him to go to bed with her; he left his coat in her hand and ran out of the room. When her husband came home, in a fit of rage, she lied to him saying that Joseph had tried to seduce her—after all— she had the "proof"! She held out the coat.

Joseph was arrested, thrown in prison and had no one to help him. But he had his dream. He didn't give up.

Soon he was put in charge of all the prisoners, and began interpreting their dreams. When one particular dream was fulfilled, the pardoned prisoner promised to tell Pharaoh about Joseph. But he forgot. Two years went by: waiting, waiting, waiting. Only his dream gave Joseph the strength to go on.

And then, one day, when God had done his perfect work in Joseph's heart, Pharaoh had a double-dream. When none of the wise men could interpret it, the pardoned prisoner remembered Joseph and told the king about him. Within the hour Joseph stood before Pharaoh and before the day was over he was elevated to being the head man over all the king's affairs—only the king was above him in rank. He had wealth, honour, dignity—everything.

All because he held on to his dream. He refused to sell his soul to Ashtoreth for a "mess of pottage." He stayed true to the commandments of holiness and obedience. By honouring God's Word, God honoured him. You **can** overcome Ashtoreth!

Chapter 13

Has God Given You a Dream?

There **is** a star we can hitch to. There **is** a dream we can dream.

In the early 1800's William Wilberforce worked for twenty years to free the slaves of England. The world mocked him. They scoffed at him. They made fun of him, even though he was a member of the British Parliament. He was a wealthy young man, who could have lived a life of ease and comfort, but he laid his life on the altar for the freeing of the slaves. He made England the first nation to free all slaves. He had a "dream."

In 1963 Martin Luther King, Jr., an American clergyman and Negro civil rights leader said, "I have a dream." His dream was to see the emancipation of all black people in the United States; that they would "live in a nation where they will not be judged by the colour of their skin but by the content of their character." No one thought his "dream" would come to pass so soon.

What is your dream? Is it for yourself—to own oil wells somewhere in Texas? That's a cheap dream. What is your dream? Is it your dream to emancipate your nation? How high is your dream? It is good to be a schoolteacher, nurse or a doctor. It's good to help society. But are you willing to go to the uttermost parts of the earth for the rest of your life, knowing that you will be misunderstood, not trusted, rejected, beaten, and even put to death? Can you go out there with humility, and not get paid for it? Are you doctors willing to forsake your six-digit salary, when you could perform a fifty thousand dollar operation comfortably here at home, to leave all to save lives for no pay—no paycheck to bring home after you have poured out your strength?

We need to remember; it is really the things you don't see that are worthwhile in this world. The things that you see are not of greatest value because they are temporal. Often today's newest fad is tomorrow's joke. It is impossible to keep up with the latest technology. Everything that is tangible is not valuable very long—just for a very little time. Nothing is lasting—except souls.

Many times, while serving God on the mission field, I would pick up my accordion and sing that beautiful missionary song written by E. Margaret Carlson:

So Send I You

So send I you—to labor unrewarded,
To serve unpaid, unloved, unsought, unknown,
To bear rebuke, to suffer scorn and scoffing—
So send I you, to toil for Me alone.

So send I you—to bind the bruised and broken,
O'er wandering souls to work, to weep, to wait,
To bear the burden of a world aweary—
So send I you, to suffer for My sake.

So send I you—to loneliness and longing,
With heart a-hungering for the loved and known,
Forsaking home, and kindred, friend and dear ones—
So send I you, to know My love alone.

So send I you—to leave your life's ambition,
To die to dear desire, self-will resign,
To labour long, and love where men revile you—
So send I you to lose your life in Mine.

So send I you—to hearts made hard by hatred,
To eyes made blind because they will not see,
To spend, though it be blood, to spend and spare not—
So send I you, to taste of Calvary.

So send I you—by grace made strong to triumph
O'er hosts of Hell, or darkness, death and sin
My name to bear, and in that name to conquer—
So send I you, My victory to win.

So send I you—to take to souls in bondage
The word of truth that sets the captive free,
To break the bonds of sin, to loose death's fetters—
So send I you, to bring the lost to Me.

So send I you—My strength to know in weakness,
My joy in grief, My perfect peace in pain,
To prove My power, My grace, My promised presence—
So send I you, eternal fruit to gain.

So send I you—to bear my cross with patience,
And then one day with you, to lay it down
To hear My voice, "Well done, My faithful servant—
Come, share My throne, My kingdom, and My crown!

As the Father hath sent me, so send I you.

Conclusion

We have come to the time that Daniel prophesied about in Daniel 12:1: *"And at that time shall Michael stand up, the great prince which standeth for the children of thy people: and there shall be a time of trouble, such as never was since there was a nation even to that same time: and at that time thy people shall be delivered, every one that shall be found written in the book."*

Jeremiah also prophesied about this time in Jeremiah 30:7, *"Alas! for that day is great, so that none is like it: it is even the time of Jacob's trouble; but he shall be saved out of it."*

There will be warfare in the heavens and on the earth, such as we have never known. That is why God has brought you here for this time. He has allowed you to go through experiences which have made you the person you are. He knows that you will be strong for the day of battle. He knows you have learned how to trust God and have faith for the hard times. He knows that you will be strong enough to stand against the demonic principalities and powers of Satan—against Ashtoreth.

Remember, you are not alone! Michael, the great prince of God who "standeth for the children" of God shall rise up to do warfare on your behalf. Your responsibility is to stay close to the heart of God. Live a holy life of prayer and fasting, and stay separated from the things of the world that Satan would use to seduce you.

It won't be long. It will soon be over; and He has promised to "deliver us" and "save us out of it."

Always remember," 1 John 4:4 says, *"Ye are of God, little children, and have overcome them: because greater is he that is in you, than he that is in the world."*

Prayer:

Father, we are facing serious things. Life is our gift from You. Some of us have made tragedies out of our lives. But you are the God of the second chance. You are the God who can forgive us and wash us in the Blood of Jesus. The same Blood that protects us, can also wash us clean and give us an opportunity to change, to be like You. Every one of us has met Ashtoreth in our lifetime. I have met her/him more than once. But you have brought me safe this far, Lord. And I thank You! It is by Your Grace alone that I have come this far. I am not better than anyone else. You have just been so merciful to me, maybe some extra people prayed for me who didn't pray for somebody else. Right here, and right now, I bow my head and rededicate my life to You, Father God, and ask You to protect me and save me and all who read this message.

"Now unto him that is able to keep you from falling, and to present you faultless before the presence of his glory with exceeding joy, To the only wise God our Saviour, be glory and majesty, dominion and power, both now and ever. Amen" (Jude 24-25).

Appendix A
Polluted Power

This account has been recorded by Apostle Emmanuel Jibuike of Nigeria. It is a true story, and is typical of what is happening in the Church of the world today. It is being retold here in the first person as it was told by the minister who experienced these events and is being included because of its relevance to Asherah, "the lady who treads upon the sea." He said to Brother Jibuike:

"I was an evangelist in Eastern Nigeria, and I relocated to Lagos, the national capital, in the hope that I would plant a church, and it would grow rapidly, and I would soon be a successful minister. So I started a church. About two years later I had nothing to show for my efforts beyond a few members. So I visited with another minister whose church I had seen growing very rapidly. I asked him what his secret was. He laughed and asked if I really wanted to know.

"After some serious discussion he gave me an appointment for further discussions. When I called to make the appointment he said that he would go somewhere with me to meet someone who would assure that my church would grow beyond my imagination. And so we drove to Victoria Island beach in Lagos. We walked together to a place in the sea front. Then he drew a sign in the sand, stepped into it, and asked me to step in there. We stood there for a while and he spoke a few strange words and suddenly I saw myself go swiftly through waters into a beautiful palatial home. There was a beautiful woman, seated like a queen, and the whole place was decked out beautifully. My partner introduced me, and stepped back.

"This woman, queen, whatever she was, told me she knew why I came and assured me that I would have my wishes if I fulfilled her conditions; that I would have a powerful ministry packed with signs and wonders; my church would grow to 500 within a year and 5000 within five years. Her conditions were that I should get married to her, and right away we should go to bed together, and I would have to give her some souls, as she instructs me.

"I was very annoyed, and I told her so. I told her that I was already married, and there was no way I could make love to her or marry her.

"She exploded with anger, and I too, angrily stood my ground against her as we argued.

"Suddenly I saw myself at the beach shore, alone. My partner was not there, and I didn't know where he went. I went home, totally bewildered.

"It was now clear to me that I had just escaped from a terrible trap of Satan. At no point did my fellow pastor tell me clearly what his power source was, and what was the basis of his church growth. He did not mention the marine-demon-marrying queen. I was not prepared for what I encountered that day. Only God saved my life, and only He gave me the grace to resist the demands of that 'queen of the coasts' as a marrying demon is usually called.

"As I gave thanks to God for my deliverance, the Lord told me to go and warn believers to beware of the danger of entering into a church just because miracles and signs and healings are being performed in that church. And I should tell people that much of the church growth and supernatural power being flaunted around today in the churches are not from Him. Fraud. That is why I dedicated my life to the task of preaching the good news and of warning Christians of this wicked trap of Satan which is intended to draw people into his kingdom through ministers who are using polluted power."

Miracles Without the Solid Word of God

This was the account given to me by this man. He goes from place to place in Lagos, standing in the public sharing his experience and to warn believers. It is very clear today that this type of minister is dominating the landscape, particularly in the southern part of Nigeria where you have the coasts nearby, where you have many new, rapidly-expanding churches springing up. This stock-preaching is prosperity without the anchor of the solid Word of God. Miracles, signs and wonders are flaunted on billboards, and posters all over the streets. And this is what draws crowds, especially because of the economical conditions of the country, and the sufferings of the people. It is very important that this message goes out to all believers and all pastors. The hunger for power, signs, wonders and miracles is satan's trap for the end times. God save us from this trap, in Jesus name!

Appendix B

The Power of Porn: Why We Lose Our Way

by Sanford Ashley

Matt was doing well in life. His marriage was great, work was good, and his kids were thriving in school. Matt felt that he could simply put life on cruise control. But when you live on cruise control, you do not have a "grip" on your life. You will tend to go with the flow. That's when life can become difficult.

Matt thought that since he was doing the right things that he could do anything. However, 1 Corinthians 6:12 shows us that everything may not be beneficial for you (NIV). A male co-worker of Mart's always made "light-hearted" jokes at work about women. Matt would laugh just to "keep the peace" instead of telling the man how offensive he was to him. The co-worker even showed him some questionable Web sites with women who were not fully clothed. Once again, Matt never stood up to the man. He simply looked at these sites with the co-worker.

One night after work, Matt went downstairs on the computer to research a family vacation. He thought about a joke his co-worker made and remembered the Web site, so he visited it. After scouring the site for some time, he clicked on a link that led to some pornographic sites. Matt was shocked initially, but continued to look for about 1 1/2 hours. Oh, by the way, he never researched his family vacation.

This became a daily ritual for Matt. He would make excuses to his wife time and time again as to why he was on the computer so much. Matt even started sharing certain porn sites with his co-worker. They both started "feeding" each other information. Their passion for pornography simply grew beyond belief.

The one thing about God's promises is that they come with a set of conditions. "Meditate on my word day and night (condition) and you will have great success (promise)." God also says whatever is done in the dark will be exposed in the light—Matt never thought about that promise.

One day, he went to work early for a staff meeting. He had a few minutes to spare, so he went on the Internet to take a "sneak peak" at a pornographic site. Matt left his computer on when he went to get a quick cup of coffee, not realizing that his boss was also in early. Matt's boss saw the pornography on his screen. Two days later, he was fired. God's promise fulfilled.

We lose our way in life sometimes because we have lost our way with God. I talk to scores of men and many fall into the pornography trap. It does not matter the geographic location, financial situation, or ethnic background; and it applies to singles, pastors, company presidents, etc. This dragon must be slayed or it will slay you.

How does one win the battle?

There is no clear cut answer, but it all starts with God.

Here is how you get going.

1. Confess your sin to God, repent, and then start to turn from your actions. God knows what is going on anyway. Come to him asking for help.

2. Set strong boundaries. Stay completely away from the triggers that cause you to sin.

3. Get help with a "checkmate." This person is here to help you win this battle and not just to "be in your business."

4. Get in God's face daily! When scripture saturates your mind and heart, sin has no place in your life.

God wants you to live the abundant life in all areas of your life. Don't shortchange yourself and others by losing your way to pornography.

Sanford Ashley is an author, speaker, and consultant. He is the author of two books on sexual temptation and infidelity. His latest release is the booklet, "Solomon's Secrets of Negotiation." Follow him on Twitter and visit his web site at www.sanfordashley.net.

Reprinted from *The Tri-State Voice*, http://tristatevoice.com
Permission requested.

Appendix C
Keep the Paths of Righteousness

by Sharon Buss

The serpent in the Garden of Eden deceived Eve by playing on her naïvety and innocence. He made subtle suggestions to cause her to doubt her loving Heavenly Father. The hidden cunning with which he attacked her caught her off guard. The devil expected that if he could get her to eat of the forbidden fruit, that all of God's plans for mankind would be undone. God would then be obliged to put them to death because of His faithfulness to His Word. Eating that fruit was like committing spiritual suicide.

The entire kingdom of darkness is committed to repeating this downfall in every human life on the planet in all generations. Ashtoreth focuses on presenting temptation in the area of sexuality, one of the strongest-driving forces in fallen man's nature. This spirit likes to attack adolescents in particular, because she knows if she can get them to engage in any form of sexual gratification, she can prevent their promising future from ever unfolding. And if she can't succeed in destroying it completely, she does her best to warp it.

Paul speaks of this subject in several verses in 1 Corinthians 6: *"Do you not know that the unrighteous and the wrongdoers will not inherit or have any share in the kingdom of God?* ***Do not be deceived (misled): neither the impure and immoral, nor idolaters, nor adulterers, nor those who participate in homosexuality,*** *Nor cheats (swindlers and thieves), nor greedy graspers, nor drunkards, nor foulmouthed revilers and slanderers, nor extortioners and robbers* ***will inherit or have any share in the kingdom of God"*** (verses 9-10 *Amplified Bible*). The latter part of verse 13 says, *"The body is not intended for sexual immorality, but [is intended] for the Lord, and the Lord [is intended] for the body to save, sanctify, and raise it again]."*

Paul goes on to explain what happens in the unseen when a man has a sexual encounter with a prostitute: *"Do you not see and know that your bodies are members (bodily parts) of Christ (the Messiah)? Am I therefore to take the parts of Christ and make [them] parts of a prostitute? Never! Never! Or do you not know and realize that when a man joins himself to a prostitute, he becomes one body with her? The two, it is written, shall become one flesh"* (1 Corinthians 6:15-16 *Amplified Bible*).

Worship practices in pagan idolatry, as well as many rituals of witchcraft and satanism, include sexual acts to establish demonic control in the soul of the worshipper.

Every sexual act establishes a covenant between the parties.[43] A sexually promiscuous person connects his/her soul with each partner in much the same way as pouring red-coloured water together with blue-coloured water. The purple-coloured water that results is impossible to separate back to the original state. An illicit sexual union results in a tainting of the soul realm and creates a soul tie.

Thanks be to God, if you have done this, repentance and prayer can wash your sin away with the Blood of Jesus and the Lord can present you clean before His Father's throne. But you do not know the irreversible harm that can be caused when you choose to disobey the Word of God. You do not know what heights you may not be able to reach as a result of your fall or the damage that the other person's soul will receive.

Blood Covenants

When a child is conceived, it is kept protected for the nine months of its development in the warm, soft nest of blood in its mother's womb. Then when the baby is born, he/she is literally covered by the blood of his/her mother. The child is born into a blood covenant with his/her parents.

---

43   http://maranathalife.com/marriage/mar-sex1.htm

When a virgin has sex for the first time, a small amount of blood is shed as the hymen is broken. This establishes a blood covenant with that sex partner. That is why it is so important to keep your virginity until the wedding night, when the covenant vows you spoke before the congregation are sealed with a blood covenant in the marriage bed.

This is also the reason why young people become rebellious when they become sexually active. They have removed themselves from their blood covenant with their parents and established their own covenant with another. It is very difficult for them to remain under their parents' roof because they have illegitimately removed themselves from the covering of their parents' authority.

Even masturbation strains their relationship with their parents because it brings shame and guilt with it, along with an addictiveness that can be maddening. Just breaking down that wall of purity and holiness in a dedicated life even once causes a "twisting away from the light" and hiding from God. It's the natural response that Adam and Eve had when they realized they were naked and began to hide.

This change in the relationship from obedience to disobedience and rebellion draws the young person into what the book of Proverbs calls foolishness. *"A foolish son is a grief to his father, and bitterness to her that bare him"* (Proverbs 17:25). BEWARE! "Flee youthful lusts" (1 Timothy 2:22)!

Consequences

Leviticus chapters 18 and 21 spell out clearly that God forbids: incest, adultery, sex during a woman's period, homosexuality, and bestiality (sexual acts with animals). Chapter 18:24-29 explains that all these types of sexual impurity cause the land to be defiled and it will vomit out its inhabitants. It also states that *"whosoever shall commit any of these abominations, even the souls that commit them shall be cut off from among their people"* (verse 29). The devil is trying to isolate people and keep from ever reaching their "Promised Land" destiny by tempting them into sexual impurity.

Proverbs 6:20-35 gives a sound warning against adultery and *The Message Bible* puts it in today's vernacular to make it so understandable:

Good friend, follow your father's good advice; don't wander off from your mother's teachings. Wrap yourself in them from head to foot; wear them like a scarf around your neck. Wherever you walk, they'll guide you; whenever you rest, they'll guard you; when you wake up, they'll tell you what's next. For sound advice is a beacon, good teaching is a light, moral discipline is a life path. They'll protect you from wanton women, from the seductive talk of some temptress. Don't lustfully fantasize on her beauty, nor be taken in by her bedroom eyes. You can buy an hour with a whore for a loaf of bread, but a wanton woman may well eat you alive. Can you build a fire in your lap and not burn your pants? Can you walk barefoot on hot coals and not get blisters? It's the same when you have sex with your neighbor's wife: Touch her and you'll pay for it. No excuses. Hunger is no excuse for a thief to steal; When he's caught he has to pay it back, even if he has to put his whole house in hock. Adultery is a brainless act, soul-destroying, self-destructive; Expect a bloody nose, a black eye, and a reputation ruined for good. For jealousy detonates rage in a cheated husband; wild for revenge, he won't make allowances. Nothing you say or pay will make it all right; neither bribes nor reason will satisfy him.

The *Amplified* version renders verse 26 as, *"But whoever commits adultery with a woman lacks heart and understanding (moral principle and prudence); he who does it is destroying his own life."* Stepping into the trap of sexual immorality is committing spiritual suicide.

Don't Be Used to Tempt

One of the ways that we can help to stamp out the fires of lust that are burning in this generation is to dress modestly.

Following hundreds of surveys and interviews with men, Shanti Feldhahn, in her book, *For Women Only,* explains to women from a man's point of view "why it's so natural for a man to look and so hard to forget what he has seen .... First, a woman who is dressed to show off a great body is an 'eye magnet' that is incredibly difficult to avoid, and even if a man forces himself not to look, he is actually aware of her presence. Second, even when no such eye magnet is present, each man has a 'mental Rolodex' of stored images that can intrude into his thoughts without warning or can be pulled up at will.[44]

The male of most species is designed by God to be ready at all times to provide their part of the procreative process. They have to be, since God created the female to be cyclic. Consequently, it doesn't take much to put men in a sexual mode. For a man to remain godly requires an enormous effort and dedication to the Lord. Keeping their thought life pure and holy under the blood of Jesus can be very challenging, for even the godliest of men.

When a woman's skirt is too short or her neckline revealing, a man can't help looking and his brain is wired to recall what he sees. You have a choice what you wear, ladies. Ask the Lord to help you to choose wisely so your image doesn't end up on the mental Rolodex of your brothers in the Lord and other men

44 Shaunti Feldhahn, *For Women Only* (Colorado Springs, Multnomah Books, 2004), 111-112. www.shaunti.com. See book ads.

you meet each day. You don't want to cause them to commit adultery in their heart with you (Matthew 5:28) do you? Don't be an eye magnet! You need to understand that immodest dressing is actually a form of sexual harassment.

The End of Ashtoreth

In Revelation 19:1-3, all of Heaven is rejoicing and praising God for His just and true judgments on the great whore, or notorious prostitute, that has corrupted the earth with her fornication. That sure sounds like Ashtoreth!

In the above paragraph, "fornication" is translated from the Greek word *porneia,* which has all of the following meanings:

"1) illicit sexual intercourse

a) adultery, fornication, homosexuality, lesbianism, intercourse with animals etc.

b) sexual intercourse with close relatives; Lev. 18

c) sexual intercourse with a divorced man or woman; Mk. 10:11,12

2) [metaphorically] the worship of idols

a) of the defilement of idolatry, as incurred by eating the sacrifices offered to idols."[45]

---

45   http://www.blueletterbible.org/lang/lexicon/lexicon.
cfm?Strongs=G4202&t=KJV

These are all the tools of Ashtoreth that she has used to corrupt the earth to destroy it and its inhabitants. But her end is very near, and the rest of Revelation 19 tells the story of the marriage of the Lamb to His Bride who has made herself ready. This is the ultimate triumph of the Lord of Glory, to have cleansed and purified His beloved with His own Blood. She is the true bride who has learned to lean on Him for all her needs, who loves Him above her own self, who has surrendered and abandoned her will to Him, trusting in His love. As the corrupted Ashtoreth goes down, the Lord raises up His true bride.

Now is the time to throw off the temptress and let the Lord bring you into the fulness of holiness and purity as you love Him and receive His love and forgiveness, overcoming Ashtoreth and walking in the victory of the Lord.

INDEX

Good old boy 15
Gospel 62
Governmental 35, 36
Great 67
Great Britain 66
Great gathering 45
Great whore 113
Grecians 11
Greece 54, 55
Greed 15
Greek Mythology 16, 60
Greeks 52
Grove 55
Groves 52
Guide 55
Hadassah 52
Ham 59
Harlot 44
Harvest 86
Hate 15
Hatred 71
Head man 91
Heaven 30
Heavenly estate 10
Hebrew 90
Hebrew (language) 11
Hebrew Greek Key Study Bible 11
Hebrews 51
Hebron 55, 56
Hell 9, 10, 13, 14, 22, 34, 36, 41,
42, 44, 76, 80, 95
High places 55
Hitler 61
Holiness 35, 113
Holy 112
Homosexuality 107, 110, 113
Hong Kong 57, 58
Honourable 57
Horns 53, 59
Horsemen 9
Hotel 58, 63

Hur 23
Husband 20, 21
Hut 29
Hymen 109
Hypnosis 16
Ichabod 66
Idol worship 113
Idolatrous 57
Idolatrous worship 56
Illicit 113
Image 56
Imaginations 87
Immodest dressing 113
Immoral 15, 55, 56, 107
Immorality 111
Incest 110
India 19
Innocent 12
Insanity 16
Instructors 45
Intercessor 20, 22, 23, 77
Intercessors 24
Animals 113
International 15
Internet 18, 36, 104
Intoxicated 44
Intoxication 57
Inventions 10
Iraq War 13
Isaac 24
Isaiah 64
Ishtar 52, 53
Isis 52
Islam 53
Isle of Patmos 9
Israel 65
Israelites 23, 80
Itching ears 5
Jacob 89-91, 97
Japan-China War 13
Jehu 81-84

Recommended Reading

Aimee - Life story of Aimee Semple McPherson. Read the autobiography of one of God's great revivalists who brought the fire down in the early 1900's .... #039401 $7.95

Authentic Annals of the Early Hebrews, The Book of Jasher. This book has all the earmarks of the genuine Book of Jasher mentioned in Joshua 10:13 and II Samuel 1:17. It provides insight into a number of biblical episodes that are otherwise unclear. It establishes an important time relationship for biblical accounts .... #107201 $19.95

Daughter of Destiny: Kathryn Kuhlman *by Jamie Buckingham.* The story of the redhead from Missouri who became the foremost woman evangelist of the 20th century. Read not of a plaster saint, but a very human person - of marriage and divorce, of betrayal within her own staff, and the glorious ministry of healing that the Holy Spirit poured out through her .... #014401 $13.99

Demons - An Eye Witness Account *by Howard Pittman.* When he died, God allowed him to visit the abode of demons and return to expose them .... #092004 $5.00

For Men Only *by Shaunti Feldhahn.* What you need to know about the inner lives of women. Shaunti surveyed and interviewed hundreds of men to learn how they really think so she could explain it to women. ....#041702 $14.99 (Hardcover)

For Women Only *by Jeff Feldhahn.* What you need to know about the inner lives of men. Jeff surveyed and interviewed hundreds of women to learn how they really think so he could explain it to men. ....#041701 $14.99 (Hardcover)

Hebrew/Greek Key Word Study Bible *complied and edited by Spiros Zodhiates, Th.D.* KJV with study system. Key words are identified with Strong's numbers right in the text. Lexical aids and Strong's Dictionary enable you to dig for deeper meanings to key words. A must for the serious student of the Word of God.

Bonded Leather Black... #H102-65 $69.99
Bonded Leather Burgundy .... #H102-66 $69.99
Genuine Leather Black .... #H102-67 $79.99
Genuine Leather Burgundy .... #H102-68 $79.99

The Nephilim Agenda *by Randy Demain.* Ancient mysteries of the Bible are unfolding with startling clarity. One such mystery is the Genesis six account of giants on the earth. These giants-the Nephilim-were the vile offspring of earthly women and divine beings bent on the deception and destruction of God's holy people .... #033926 $15.00

A Soldier in Vietnam *by Roger Sprinkle.* In two sessions Roger shared story after story of his experiences in Vietnam, showing God's often miraculous care on the battle field. 2CDs ....#RS1-YR07C $10.00
DVD ....#RS1-YR07D $12.00
2nd meeting, 1 CD .... #RS2-YR07C CD $7.00
DVD ....#RS2-YR07D $12.00

Vietnam Testimony *by Roger Sprinkle.* This is a very moving testimony of a young sergeant who served in Vietnam during the war. Available in CD or DVD as recorded in the End-Time Handmaidens Winter Camp Meeting.................................#RS1-WM08C CD $7.00
.... #RS1-WM08D DVD $12.00

"Overcoming Ashtoreth" *by Gwen Shaw.* This message was preached at the Anointed Youth Winter Retreat. CD..........#GS1-AY07C $7.00
DVD ....#GS1-AY07D $12.00

"Ashtoreth" *by Gwen Shaw.* This message was preached at the End-Time Handmaidens Winter Camp. 2 CDs.......#GS2-WM08C $10.00
DVD ....#GS2-WM08D $12.00

More Books by Gwen Shaw

UNCONDITIONAL SURRENDER. The life story of Gwen R. Shaw, lovingly known as "Sister Gwen" to thousands of people in over one hundred nations. Feel the heartbeat of a great woman of God who has given all to Him, asking only for souls in return. Your life will be challenged as you walk with her through mission field after mission field. You will never be the same when you read how God pours out His Spirit and confirms His Word. Paperback ....#000102 $14.00
DVD NTSC (North American format)...#DGSN $15.00
DVD PAL (European format) ....#DGSP $15.00

Daily Devotionals

DAILY PREPARATIONS FOR PERFECTION — This daily devotional comes to you exactly as the Holy Spirit spoke to the author's heart in her own private devotions. You will feel that Jesus is speaking to you every time you open it. It is loved by all. You'll read it and re-read it .... Paperback #000202 $12.50

DAY BY DAY— This daily devotional book based on the Psalms will give you an inspiring word directly from the Throne Room each day to fill your heart with praise to God. Starting each day with praise is the secret of a joy-filled life .... Softcover #000204 $11.95 Hardcover #000203 $18.50

FROM THE HEART OF JESUS — Walk and talk with Jesus as he ministered, as He suffered and died and as He rose again from the dead. These words from the heart of Jesus will go straight to your heart, bringing comfort, peace, encouragement and hope! 923 pages .... Hardcover #000207 $29.95

GEMS OF WISDOM — *A daily devotional based on the book of Proverbs.* Find instruction in the Proverbs for upright living, honesty, justice and wisdom. Every word applies to today's problems as when they were first written. If you are going through great difficulties and facing problems which seem to have no solution, you will find the answer in these Proverbs. Hardcover #000209 $25.95

HE SENT ME BACK TO TELL YOU *by Gwen Saw.* While Sister Gwen's body was in intensive care, her spirit was standing at the gates of Heaven. The intercessors begged God to send her back. He heard their cries and returned her to earth with a message... #000213 $37.95

IN THE BEGINNING — *A daily devotional based on the book of Genesis.* The Book of Genesis is the foundation stone of all knowledge and wisdom. Deep and wonderful truths hidden in the pages of Genesis are revealed in this devotional book. Hardcover .... #000211 $27.95

Bible Studies

BEHOLD THE BRIDEGROOM COMETH! A Bible study on the soon return of Jesus Christ. With so many false teachings around, it is important to realize how imminent the rapture of the saints of God really is ... #000304 $6.50

ENDUED WITH LIGHT TO REIGN FOREVER. This deeply profound Bible study reveals the characteristics of the eternal, supernatural, creative light of God as found in His Word. ....#000306 $5.00

GOD'S END-TIME BATTLE-PLAN. This study on spiritual warfare gives you the biblical weapons for spiritual warfare such as victory through dancing, shouting, praising, uplifted hands, marching, etc...........................#000305 $8.00

IT'S TIME FOR REVIVAL. A Bible study on revival that gives scriptural promises of the end-time revival, and stories of revivals in the past. It will stir your heart and encourage you to believe for great revival! ....#000311 $7.75

OUR MINISTERING ANGELS. Angels will be playing a more and more prominent part in these last days. We need to understand about them and their ministry. Read exciting accounts of angelic help...........................#000308 $8.00

POUR OUT YOUR HEART. A wonderful Bible study on travailing prayer. The hour has come to intercede before the throne of God. The call to intercession is for everyone, and we must carry the Lord's burden and weep for the lost so that the harvest can be brought in quickly .... #000301 $5.00

REDEEMING THE LAND. A Bible study on spiritual warfare. This important teaching will help you know your authority through the Blood of Jesus to dislodge evil spirits, break the curse, and restore God's blessing upon the land .... #000309 $9.50

THE FINE LINE. This Bible study clearly magnifies the "fine line" of difference between the soul realm and the spirit realm. Both are intangible and therefore cannot be discerned with the five senses, but must be discerned by the Holy Spirit and the Word of God. A must for the deeper Christian .... #000307 $6.00

THE POWER OF THE PRECIOUS BLOOD. A Bible study on the Blood of Jesus. The author shares how it was revealed to her how much Satan fears Jesus' Blood. This Bible study will help you overcome and destroy the works of Satan in your life and the lives of loved ones! .... #000303 $5.00

THE POWER OF PRAISE. When God created the heavens and the earth, He was surrounded by praise. Miracles happen when holy people praise a Holy God! Praise is the language of creation. If prayer can move the hand of God, how much more praise can move Him! .... #000312 $5.00

YE SHALL RECEIVE POWER FROM ON HIGH. This is a much needed foundational teaching on the Baptism of the Holy Spirit. It will enable you to teach this subject, as well as to understand these truths more fully yourself .... #000310 $5.00

YOUR APPOINTMENT WITH GOD. A Bible study on fasting. Fasting is one of the most neglected sources of power over bondages of Satan that God has given the Church. This Bible study will change your life............. #000302 $5.00

FORGIVE AND RECEIVE. This Bible Study is a lesson to the church on the much-needed truths of forgiveness and restoration. The epistle to Philemon came from the heart of Paul who had experienced great forgiveness.... #000406 $7.00

MYSTERY REVEALED. Search the depths of God's riches in one of Paul's most profound epistles, "to the praise of His glory!" Learn the "mystery" of the united Body of Christ as revealed in the book of Ephesians ...... #000403 $15.00

THE CATCHING AWAY! This is a very timely Bible study because Jesus is coming soon! The book of 1 Thessalonians explains God's revelation to Paul on the rapture of the saints. 2 Thessalonians reveals what will happen after the rapture when the antichrist takes over .... #000407 $13.00

THE TRIBES OF ISRAEL. This popular and well-loved study on the thirteen tribes of Israel will show you your place in the spiritual tribes in these last days. Understand yourself and others better through the study of this Bible Course! ....#000501 $45.00 • 13 CD set - #CTGS1 $50.00

Women of the Bible Series

EVE—MOTHER OF US ALL. Read the life story of the first woman. Discover the secrets of one of the most misunderstood stories in history .... #000801 $4.50

SARAH—PRINCESS OF ALL MANKIND. She was beautiful — and barren. Feel the heartbeat and struggles of this great woman...................... #000802 $4.50

REBEKAH—THE BRIDE. The destiny of the world was determined when she said three simple words, "I will go!" Enjoy this touching story. .... #000803 $4.50

LEAH AND RACHEL—THE TWIN WIVES OF JACOB. You will feel their dreams, their pains, their jealousies and their love for one man.... #000804 $4.50

MIRIAM—THE PROPHETESS. Miriam was the first female to lead worship, the first woman to whom the Lord gave the title "Leader of God's people." .... #000805 $7.50

DEBORAH AND JAEL. May God's "warrior women" now arise to take their place in the end-time battle for the harvest! .... #000806 $4.50

Other Books by Gwen Shaw

GOING HOME. Prepare hearts for Heaven and bring comfort to loved ones. Receive strength and faith when facing death. It's a book about Going Home to our Eternal Abode to be with our loving Heavenly Father ....#000607 $8.00

LOVE, THE LAW OF THE ANGELS. This is undoubtedly the greatest of Gwen Shaw's writings. It carries a message of healing and life in a sad and fallen civilization. Love heals the broken-hearted and sets disarray in order. You will never be the same after reading this beautiful book about love .#000601 $10.00

SONG OF LOVE. She was heart-broken, far from home and cried out to God for help. He spoke, "Turn to the Song of Solomon and read!" The Lord took her into the "Throne Room" of Heaven and taught her about the love of Christ for His Bride. Fall in love with Jesus afresh ....#000401 $8.95

TO BE LIKE JESUS. Based on her Throne Room experience in 1971, the author shares the Father's heart about our place as sons in His Family. Nothing is more important than *To Be Like Jesus*!...#000605 $8.00

Prices are subject to change.
For a complete catalogue with current pricing, contact:

Engeltal Press
P.O. Box 447 • Jasper, ARK 72641 U.S.A.
Telephone (870) 446-2665 • Fax (870) 446-2259
Email books@eth-s.org • Website www.engeltalpress.com